W9-BEG-921

PENGUIN BOOKS
THE JOY IN LOVING

Agnes Bojaxhiu, or Mother Teresa as the world knows her today, was born on 26 August 1910, in Yugoslavia. In 1928 she left home to become a novice of Loreto and in 1931 she arrived in India, where she took religious vows of poverty, chastity, and obedience and was renamed Teresa. After teaching at St. Mary's School in Calcutta for several years, Mother started the Congregation of the Missionaries of Charity, which was approved by a decree of the Holy See in 1950. Since then, the congregation has expanded to include more than six hundred Homes in as many as a hundred and thirty-six countries. She has been the recipient of several prestigious awards, including the Nobel Peace Prize. Mother Teresa passed away on 5 September 1997.

*

Jaya Chaliha works with underprivileged women and children in Calcutta. She began writing when she was fifty-two years old and has contributed travelogues and articles on a wide range of subjects for newspapers, magazines, and anthologies. She has known Mother Teresa since the 1960s and has worked with her Sisters from time to time.

*

Father Edward Le Joly, born in Liège, Belgium, on 11 August 1909, studied law, joined the Society of Jesus to become a priest and missionary, and came to India in 1937. After his ecclesiastical studies he lectured on economics at St. Xavier's College, Calcutta. Fourteen years later he went to a city parish as assistant and writer of spiritual books.

When Mother Teresa started her Missionaries of Charity, she asked him to help her train her Sisters. For thirty years he gave the Sisters spiritual instruction. Mother Teresa also asked him to write the true story of her foundation. This book, *We Do It for Jesus*, was published in fourteen languages. In all, Father Le Joly has written twenty-five books. The last, *The Call of Jesus*, is an autobiography.

The
Joy
in
Loving

A GUIDE TO DAILY LIVING WITH

Mother
Teresa

COMPILED BY JAYA CHALIHA & EDWARD LE JOLY

PENGUIN BOOKS

Penguin Books India (P) Ltd., 210, Chiranjiv Tower, 43, Nehru Place,
New Delhi 110 019, India
Penguin Books Ltd., 27 Wrights Lane, London W8 5TZ, UK
Penguin Books USA Inc., 375 Hudson Street, New York, New Yark 10014, USA
Penguin Books Australia Ltd., Ringwood, Victoria, Australia
Penguin Books Canada Ltd., 10 Alcorn Avenue, Suite 300, Toronto, Ontario M4V 3B2, Canada
Penguin Books (NZ) Ltd., 182-190 Wairau Road, Auckland 10, New Zealand

First published in VIKING by Penguin Books India (P) Ltd. 1996
Published in Penguin Books 1997

Copyright © Jaya Chaliha and Edward Le Joly 1996

Sayings reproduced by kind permission of Mother Teresa and the Missionaries of Charity

Worldwide royalties from *The Joy in Loving* have been assigned to the Missionaries of Charity.

All rights reserved

10 9 8 7 6 5 4 3 2 1

Typeset in Garamond by FOLIO, New Delhi-110001
Printed at Rekha Printers Pvt. Ltd., New Delhi-110020

This book is sold subject to the condition that it shall not, by way of trade or otherwise, be lent, resold,
hired out, or otherwise circulated without the publisher's prior written consent in any form of
binding or cover other than that in which it is published and without a similar condition including
this condition being imposed on the subsequent purchaser and without limiting the rights under
copyright reserved above, no part of this publication may be reproduced, stored in or introduced into
a retrieval system, or transmitted in any form or by any means (electronic, mechanical, photocopying,
recording or otherwise), without the prior written permission of both the copyright owner and the
above-mentioned publisher of this book.

Mother Teresa
Superior General
Missionaries of Charity

On the happy occasion of your forthcoming Birthday I join all the Missionaries of Charity in thanking Almighty God for the witness of your religious consecration and your untiring service of the poorest of the poor.

As a pledge of strength and joy in our Lord and Saviour Jesus Christ, I gladly impart my Apostolic Blessing.

IOANNES PAULUS PP. II
22 April 1996

Dear,

Keep the joy of loving
Jesus in your heart.
And share this joy with
all you meet especially
your family.

Let us pray
God bless you
M Teresa mc

CONTENTS

ACKNOWLEDGEMENTS

Thank you for your contributions in so many different ways :

Archbishop Henry D'Souza, Archbishop of Calcutta; Sisters, Missionaries of Charity, Mother House, Calcutta; Miss Jacquline de Decker, International Link of the suffering co-workers of Mother Teresa; Mr Arinrajit T. Chaliha; Mr Indrajit Chaliha; Ms Joyoti Chaliha; Ms Renuka Chatterjee; co-workers of Mother Teresa, Calcutta; Ms Eilen Eagen; Mrs Sohinder Grewal; Father A Huart S.J. and Mrs Tara Sinha.

For kind permission to reprint material, we thank the following :

Archives, Missionaries of Charity, Mother House, Calcutta; Alba House, New York, for excerpt from *For the Least of My Brothers* by Fr. Omar Tanghe; Harpercollins Publishers Inc. for excerpt from *Mother Teresa : Her People and Her Work* by Desmond Doig and *Love Until It Hurts* by Daphne Rae; Navin Chawla for excerpts from *Mother Teresa* published by Gulmohar Press Pvt. Ltd.; and St. Paul's, Bombay, for excerpts from *We Do It for Jesus, Mother Teresa : Messenger of God's Love* and *Mother Teresa : The Glorious Years* by Fr. E. Le Joly S.J.

Mother Teresa lay critically ill in a Calcutta nursing home in August 1996. People all over the world prayed for her recovery. In Calcutta thousands visited the chapel in Mother House to join her Sisters in silent prayer.

The Joy in Loving was compiled and published for a birthday gift to Mother Teresa on the occasion of her eighty-sixth anniversary on 26 August. We were happy that His Holiness Pope John Paul II had acceded to our request made through the Archbishop of Calcutta for a birthday message to Mother Teresa which appears on the first page of the book. Would Mother receive our gift, we wondered.

On the morning of 24 August 1996, after a night of great suffering, Mother whispered to one of her Sisters:

'I don't know what God is doing,
He knows
We do not understand
But one thing I'm sure
He doesn't make a mistake.'

Mother returned home. A short while later she was admitted to a well-known Heart Centre in the city. At about the same time, Sister Agnes, her first aspirant to the Missionaries of Charity was seriously ill. In her holiness, Sister Agnes is said to have prayed that Mother may be spared to continue her work for a little longer. Mother's recovery was miraculous. Sister Agnes died and Mother was at her graveside.

To add to her work, Mother Teresa autographed many, many copies of *The Joy in Loving*, and always with a smile.

In February 1997, she blessed Sister Nirmala, her elected successor as Superior General of the Order which she had founded forty-seven years ago. She travelled to Rome and to the Homes she had established in the USA and returned to Calcutta in July 1997.

Mother Teresa passed away peacefully on 5 September, 1997 at Mother House, Calcutta. In an unprecedented departure from protocol, the Indian government honoured Mother with a state funeral. In the words of Fr Edward Le Joly (S.J.), Mother Teresa was not just a great international figure, she was the event of this half-century.

Calcutta   *Jaya Chaliha*
17-9-1997

Teresa is her name in religion. At home she was called Agnes, her baptismal name.

Agnes Bojaxhiu, daughter of Nicolas and Rosa, sister of Agata and Lazarus, was born on 26 August, 1910 at Skoplje in Yugoslavia, and baptized on 27 August, 1910.

The Bojaxhiu family belonged to the Albanian minority living in Serbia, Yugoslavia. The young Agnes never set foot in Albania. In 1920, she went to study in a State secondary school in Croatia. She heard about India and the work of the Catholic missionaries in West Bengal through letters sent by Father Antony Vizjak, a Jesuit missionary. This made her wish to come to Bengal as a missionary. Learning that the Loreto nuns from Ireland worked in Calcutta, she decided to go to Dublin and apply to join them. On 26 September, 1928, Agnes left her home and travelled to Ireland to become a novice of Loreto. She was well received in Dublin and at her request was soon sent as a young novice to the missions in India.

She arrived in Calcutta on 6 January, 1929 and was sent to the novitiate of the Loreto nuns at Darjeeling, at the foot of the Himalayas. In 1931, Agnes took the religious vows of poverty, chastity and obedience and changed her name to Teresa.

She was sent to teach at St. Mary's High School in Entally, Calcutta, which catered to middle-class Bengali girls. She later became the headmistress of the school.

On 10 September, 1946, which is observed by the congregation as 'Inspiration Day', as she travelled by train to Darjeeling, Mother Teresa was told by Jesus : 'I want you to serve Me among the poorest of the poor.' This inspiration changed her life. She knew she had to leave Loreto and her teaching and devote her life to work and prayer among the very poor. She was sure it was an order from the Lord.

In 1948, Mother applied to Rome for the privilege of exclaustration — living outside the convent — and it was granted to her. She then went to Patna for a crash course in medical aid at the hospital of the American Medical Missionaries Sisters. On returning to Calcutta she stayed for some time at the Home of the Little Sisters of the Poor and worked in the slums.

In February 1949, Mother Teresa was welcomed by Mr Michael Gomes who put at her disposal first a room, then the entire top floor of his large house. On 19 March, a young lady, who later took the religious name Agnes, came to tell Mother, 'I want to join you.' Mother said, 'It will be hard.' The young lady answered, 'I know. I am prepared.' And she stayed with Mother.

Soon the girls who had been Mother's pupils at St. Mary's came to offer themselves as candidates. Along with Mother, they prayed and went to work teaching poor children in the slums.

As the number of young ladies wishing to work with Mother increased, it became clear that God wanted her to start a new religious congregation. So Mother began to draft the Constitution of the Missionaries of Charity, the name she had chosen for her Sisters. After two years of training in a novitiate, the candidates were to take the vows of religion, namely poverty, chastity and obedience, as all other religious men and women do. Mother added a fourth vow of 'wholehearted free service to the poorest of the poor.'

This fourth vow that all the Missionaries of Charity take is an essential element of their institute, which can never be dropped or changed without the congregation losing its identity. Mother introduced it and made it binding forever because she knew that several congregations that had initially worked for the poor had gradually become schools for the well-to-do. She did not want this to happen with her Sisters.

The draft of the Constitution was sent to Rome for approval. On 7 October 1950, by a decree from the Holy See, the Congregation of the Missionaries of Charity and their Constitution received approval. From then on, the number of vocations increased steadily.

On 22 August, 1952 the Home for the Dying was opened at Kalighat and also the Home for Children. The Sisters worked regularly in these two Homes.

In 1953 Mother and twenty-eight Sisters left the house of Michael Gomes which had become too small for the group and went to occupy a house at 54 A, Lower Circular Road (A.J.C.Bose Road) which became, and still is, the Mother House of the Congregation.

Mother has a great trust in prayer and suffering offered to God. From the start she wished that she and every one of her Sisters be linked with a sick or suffering person. She once expressed this desire to a young Belgian lady, Miss Jacqueline de Decker who had come to India but was unable to join Mother in her work due to illness.

One day, as Miss de Decker was praying in Bangalore, she heard a Voice asking her : 'Are you ready to suffer so that another can do the work?' She was to offer her pain and suffering for Mother's work. She did it and continues to do so, even today. She is in charge of the International Sick and Suffering wing of the Missionaries of Charity, each of whose members is linked to an active Sister, praying for her holiness and apostolate.

Mother also wished to organize for prayer

and work the generous lay persons who contributed money, food and medicines for her work among the poor. Soon, donors started coming forward, as also helpers for the work.

A Chinese lady, Mrs Chater sent her driver with the car daily, to take the young novices from the Gomes house to the Home for the Dying at Kalighat. She also sent cooked food for the sick. Some ladies came to work at the Children's Home as part-time helpers. There was a need to channelize the good will of many, to organize the helpers for prayer and work : this gave birth to the Co-workers of the Missionaries of Charity.

The Co-workers were for Mother a welcome means of spreading her message of God's love. Started in Calcutta, they gradually spread their network throughout the world. Mrs Ann Blaikie was for many years the movement's main speaker and organizer in several countries.

From the early days of the Society, the Missionaries of Charity attracted people from every part of the world who wished to have some part in the work of loving service to God in the person of the needy. Out of this grew the International Association of the Co-workers of Mother Teresa. Mother Teresa presented a Constitution of the Association to Pope Paul VI who gave his blessing on 29

March, 1969. It was then affiliated with the Society of the Missionaries of Charity. Mother defined what a Co-worker should be : 'My prayer for you is that you may grow in the likeness of Christ, that you be real carriers of God's love and that you really bring his presence, first, into your own family, then, to the next door neighbour, the street we live in, the town we live in, the country we live in, then only, in the whole world, that living example of God's presence.'

Mother had been told by the Archbishop to not start any work outside Calcutta for ten years, but to concentrate on training her nuns and moulding future Superiors of houses. She did so.

In 1963 started the expansion which never slowed down and is still in full swing, as more houses are being opened and more nuns being trained.

In 1963 Mother opened houses in Ranchi, Jhansi, Delhi and Bombay. In 1964 Pope Paul VI came to Bombay for the International Eucharist Congress and, among other things, shared a breakfast with the orphan children in the home of the Missionaries of Charity. Before returning to Rome, he gave Mother the white Lincoln limousine in which he had motored through Bombay. Mother did not sell the car; her friends raffled it and collected five times its value.

In 1965, Mother was happy : 'We opened a house in Venezuela, the first in the Americas,' she said. 'Yes, Mother, there is a huge field for your work in Latin America,' I said.

In 1967, at the express request of Pope Paul VI, Mother opened a house and a novitiate on the outskirts of Rome. She was received by the Pope in his study in the Vatican, and there was no protocol. They were alone and 'I talked to him as I talk to you now,' she said.

In the following years, foundations multiplied at an increased tempo : in India, Australia, Melbourne, Jordan, Gaza and North Yemen. Then in Ethiopia, Tanzania, Philippines, New Guinea, Belgium, Germany, Holland, United States, Colombia, Peru, Fiji, Papua etc. Mother said : 'We have applications from more than one hundred bishops all over the world.'

'How do you select the winners?' I asked.

'We go where the needs are greater,' she replied.

'That is a fair criterion. And you have experience regarding needs.'

When we celebrated the twenty-fifth anniversary of the Society, many priests thought the right policy would be to stop expanding and work to consolidate the existing foundations and train Superiors.

I asked : 'Mother, are you going to stop expanding in order to strengthen the existing foundations?'

Mother replied : 'We had the Jubilee of our Society, the Jubilee of the Home for the Dying, the Jubilee of the Children's Home, the Jubilee of the work for the leprosy patients.

'Father, next year we shall have the Jubilee of Jesus. I will open twenty-five houses where Jesus will live and be loved and served in the poor.' Mother, in love with Jesus, was offering him a wonderful gift.

'Mother, you are right, you have the wind of God's grace in your sails, make the most of it,' I said.

The twenty-five houses were opened, and Mother was filled with joy. 'And next year,' she said, 'I will open twenty-five more houses to make it the Golden Jubilee of Jesus.' And she did it.

Every year has seen, and still sees, Mother starting new foundations. At the time of writing, there are six hundred houses in 136 countries. And there are still many applications from bishops on the waiting list.

How can such success be explained? In human terms at least, it is impossible to do so. 'It is all God's work,' says Mother, taking no credit for herself.

Mother wished to bring young men to

join her apostalate. They would be able to look after the street boys, the orphans without shelter, the boys who ran away from school and from home. She knew she couldn't train the candidates herself, having her hands full already; she needed an experienced priest for that task.

God sent her a Jesuit priest, Father Andrew Travers-Ball, an Australian missionary in India. Brother Andrew, as he was later called, was released from the Society of Jesus and started the Missionaries of Charity (M.C.) Brothers. Many young men came to join him. He became the General Servant for the new institute, wrote the Constitution of the Brothers and trained young men who became novices to prepare for their vows.

The M.C. Brothers increased in numbers and set up several foundations in India, in Madagascar, in South Korea and a few other countries. They are stabilized at about four hundred members. Later, Mother started a contemplative wing among the M.C. Sisters to concentrate on prayer and contemplation and do some spiritual work outside their convents. She also started with Brother Sebastian, a priest, the Brothers of the Word. These are priests and Brothers living as contemplatives and spreading the word of God in the world.

For good measure, Mother inspired and

established, with Father Langford, the Society of the Missionaries of Charity Priests who do spiritual work among the poorest of the poor.

For Mother, Jesus is everything — the beginning, the middle and the end of her work, of her whole enterprise. There is no need to seek elsewhere, for Jesus explains all that has been done. Mother claims no credit for herself. On the contrary, she says : 'I don't do it, he does it. I am only an instrument in his hand. I am surer of this than of my own life.'

All Christians believe that God is present in the soul of the baptized by grace. A few persons totally dedicated to God are even granted the experience of the divine Presence, a state that is beautifully described by Brother Lawrence in his book, *The Presence of God*.

Mother also says : 'I see Jesus in the poor.' Again, she sees him, not only by faith as all believers do, since he said : 'What you do to the least of mine, you do it unto me', but by a mystical experience.

It may be recalled that some saints and holy persons attending on the sick and the dying poor, such as St. Camillus de Lellis, were conscious of Jesus being in them. This was a gift of God to reward their generous love and service.

'God has made me a great gift,' said Mother, 'he gave me a strong constitution.'

Indeed she needs it, because her style of life is spartan. Up at 4 a.m. every day, she is in the chapel by the time the Sisters get up at 4.30 a.m. She prays and follows the holy Mass which starts for the whole community at 6 a.m. She always ate very little; now hardly anything, a few biscuits soaked in tea. Her small room, serving as her office, is the hottest in the house, being situated just above the kitchen. There is a small window and of course, no fan. So, in the hot months it is less than pleasant.

Mother prays and works the whole day, writing letters till late into the night, despite the fact that she has suffered three serious hearts attacks that kept her in bed for several weeks. The best doctors had attended on her in Calcutta, Rome, New York. At present she suffers from angina pectoris and carries a pace-maker. At the age of 85, she still accepts speaking assignments and travels a great deal.

Mother Teresa said : 'God's greatest grace to me has been to send me suffering so that I could be similar to Jesus dying on the cross out of love for us.' To suffer with Christ for the Church, in the words of St. Francis of Assisi, is perfect joy, because it is perfect love. But few are the souls who experience that joy.

Mother Teresa does not seek popularity, neither does she shun it. During an interview with a Japanese editor of a leading newspaper, she said, 'Mr. Kato, you write so well, please write in your newspaper : Mother Teresa needs a house, a nice house. The Japanese are rich. A person owning two houses can give one.' Who but Mother Teresa could have said that!

And it is true that the media helped Mother Teresa to become what she is and in the process made her a media star. Had she not been constantly in the news, she could not have opened six hundred houses in over one hundred and thirty countries and still have no debt.

The Calcutta daily, *The Statesman* was the first to publicize her work in this city. Later, Malcolm Muggeridge came to Calcutta to make a film on the life of the Sisters. As the crew got ready to start filming in the Mother House, Mother Teresa exclaimed : 'Let us do something beautiful for God.' The words summarize her life and work; they have become a clarion call to action and holiness. The film itself won acclaim in the U.K.

The many international prizes and awards given to Mother Teresa were like steps that helped her climb the ladder to celebrity and stardom.

First, the Magsaysay Award in Manila, then the Templeton Prize in England, the

Nobel Peace Prize in Oslo, the Bharat Ratna, the highest civilian decoration in India and the Kennedy Prize in the U.S.

At the screening of the film *Mother Teresa* at the Fortieth Anniversary of the UN, the General Secretary, Javier Perez de Cuellar presented her to the gathering with the words : 'I introduce to you the most powerful woman in the world.'

Time magazine called her 'a loving saint' and the New York Governor added : 'She may be the only one.'

Mother Teresa has received so many awards, prizes, doctorates and citations, that she cannot keep count of them. She always says :

'It is for the honour of God and I receive this in the name of the poor and for their benefit.'

Even in the midst of work and prayer, Mother retains a sense of humour that allows her to enjoy the unexpected. She once told me with a smile : 'The Prime Minister of North Yemen, a Muslim, presented to me a Sword of Honour in recognition of the good work of our Sisters in our house for leprosy patients in his country.'

Mother has 'made' the cover of practically every important news magazine in the world. Editors, journalists and reporters have trooped to Calcutta to interview her. They have come to me, too, to ask about her and especially about the succession. 'Who will take over after her, whom has she groomed to be her successor? You know the Sisters well. Who is able enough to succeed her? Is there, as with the French, "a dauphin"? Who is your candidate? Will the M.C.s continue after Mother?'

They came from the BBC, *Time*, *Newsweek*, the Associated Press, the *Osservatore Romano*, *La Croix*, and from Japan. A lady editor of the Paris women's magazine *Elle* told me : 'I came to Delhi to write on colours in women's dresses; I might as well as do an article on Mother Teresa.'

Most of the journalists had their own ideas about why Mother Teresa had started to work among the poor in the slums. One story ran like this : Mother, while teaching rich children in her school, had seen the misery in the streets and slums of Calcutta and decided to leave her convent and start working for the downtrodden.

I told them the true story — the call of Jesus to serve him in the poorest of the poor; I thought that one from her entourage should make known what really happened. Still, Mother often complains : 'We are too much in the news. They make too much fuss about us. What we do, others do also. It's all God's work.'

So, when one day I asked, 'Mother, may I write about you and your Sisters?' I did not expect her to show any enthusiasm for my proposal. But she answered immediately : 'Father, do it. Tell them we are not here for the work, we are here for Jesus. We are religious, not social workers, not nurses, not teachers, we are religious Sisters. All we do, our prayer, our work, our suffering is for Jesus . . . . He gives me strength. I love Him in the poor and the poor in Him. Without Jesus our life would be meaningless, incomprehensible . . . .' She thumped her fist on the table and summed up, 'Father, tell them : We do it for Jesus.' I left the house happy, I had a title for my book. Mother told me, 'I do not care what they write about us; but I care what you write, because you have known us from the beginning.'

We Do it for Jesus was published in 1977 in London, New York and Calcutta and was soon translated into fourteen languages. A new edition was published by St. Paul's, Bombay in 1995. An American publisher wrote to me : 'You are the man to tell us what are the fundamental ideas of the Missionaries of Charity and what is their influence in the world.' I tried to do that, while continuing the story and thus produced a second volume : *Mother Teresa, Messenger of God's Love.* Later, when Mother was in her eighties, to bring her story up-to-date and show how God blessed her work, I wrote *Mother Teresa, the Glorious Years.* Indeed, Mother Teresa has been sent by Pope John Paul II as an ambassadress and has been received by many Heads of State, including the U.S. President. In her small parlour at Mother House, most of the important visitors to Calcutta have also come to pay their respects to this simple, smiling, loving nun.

A long-cherished hope of Mother's was abundantly fulfilled when she was finally allowed to set foot in Albania, where she soon brought in her Sisters and opened seven houses in the only country in the world that had claimed to be an 'Atheistic Republic'. Now the children could be taught to pray to God who loved them and made them to love him. A foreign reporter asked me, 'I am going to Delhi to cover the Bharat Ratna Awards ceremony. Do you think it will be possible to take a picture of Mrs Indira Gandhi and Mother Teresa talking together?' 'That will not be difficult,' I told him. 'They are both media persons. After the ceremony they will come together to meet the cameras and the press, they will talk and smile as long as you wish and you can all take films and pictures.' And so it was.

The media made it possible to spread Mother Teresa's message all over the world.

Mother has spoken thousands of times and reached hundreds of millions of listeners through radio, television, cinema and the press. 'How do you speak, Mother? Do you use notes or prepared texts?' 'Father, I make a little cross on my lips with my thumb; then I look straight forward above the audience and deliver my message.' Her talks, always easy to follow, are enlivened by moving stories of her experiences.

Her message has never changed. What she says is as steady, as universally adapted as the Holy Scripture which inspires her. The core of her message :

'God is love.

'God created all men and women out of love and he continues to love them. Therefore, we must love God and love one another as God loves us.

'Jesus Christ, the Son of God who became man and lived among us, said : "What you did to the least of mine, you did it to me." Thus, when we serve and do good to the poor, we serve and do good to Jesus.

'At the end of life we shall be judged by love, according to the love we have shown and practised towards our fellow men and women.'

Mother has always been inspired by the Sermon on the Mount. Indeed, she lives by it : 'Blessed are the poor in spirit, the little ones, the humble of heart, blessed are the gentle, the kind, the peace-makers, the merciful, the pure of heart who shall see God.'

She says : 'As God gives good things freely, so we should give freely to needy people.'

Mother develops her great themes thus :

First comes Love which must be universal, generous, effective. It starts at home and spreads in concentric circles to neighbour, street, locality, province, state, continent, world.

Then, respect for Life that comes from God, who alone can give it and take it back. Like a prophet of old, Mother thunders at the vice of abortion so prevalent in our days, and flays those who kill the unborn child in the mother's womb. Only God may know how many women decided 'no abortion' after hearing or reading Mother's appeal to their conscience to not murder an unborn child.

Then, Peace in the home, between communities, between nations. Peace requires prayer, understanding, forbearance, sharing in love.

For every person to live in love, it requires Prayer, turning to God to speak to him and listen to him. Mother suggests family prayers and has popularized Father Peyton's famous saying : 'the family that prays together stays together.' From prayer comes love, from love comes :

Service of the needy, of the poor, the sick, the suffering, the lonely, the neglected and forgotten.

The Sermon on the Mount that Jesus preached to the crowd following him, ended with the invitation, 'be perfect as your Father in heaven is perfect.' Mother therefore invites everyone to attain holiness, not reserved for a few religious persons but open to all, whatever their vocation in life.

Mother advises each one to be perfect in his line, his position, his avocation, whatever be his work. She knows that we have different functions in the world, that God gives us various gifts adapted to our state in society. Thus, she told me : 'Father, I don't want you to go and wash the dying in Kalighat, my Sisters can do that. I want you to teach them how to become good nuns, to teach them spirituality by your lectures and writing. That is your work.'

To inspire me, three times she said : 'Write meditations for my Sisters.' Three times I answered, 'I cannot do it.' Then one day I got an inspiration : the Gospel of St. John, the gospel of love. 'Yes, I will do it, not only for the Sisters, but for all lovers of God.' A year later when *Remain in my Love* was published, I gave a copy to Mother Teresa.

Three weeks later, she told me, 'Father, thank you for writing that book; I use it every day.' *Remain in my Love* is now available in ten languages. Thank you, Mother, for making me write it!

Mother is the most travelled religious foundress in history. She has visited every continent several times. Each time, she has spoken to the people who gathered to see and hear her. Airlines are proud to offer her free passage and though she asks for economy class, she is often put into business class. 'I ask for a free seat next to mine,' she says, 'so that people can come and talk to me. Eventually I ask that the curtain separating the classes be left open.' Then she shows her interest in every person, listening to their stories, giving advice, promising prayers. Wherever she goes she is invited to speak and she delivers her message, the core of which is Prayer and Love.

For her, prayer comes first, because it brings us the grace of God to love and do acts of love. So she wishes to lead all mankind in prayer.

On returning from the Fortieth Anniversary meeting of the United Nations Organization Mother told me, 'Father, it was wonderful. I made them pray in that hall where they had never prayed before. I told them : "this organization was established to promote peace in the world. Let us pray to God, the only One who can give us peace." And I led them in reciting the prayer of St. Francis of Assisi : "Lord, make me an instrument of your peace." I had friends distribute leaflets with the prayer.'

Mother's message appeals to all, whether they believe in God or not. Non-believers in God and persons not given to prayer can open their hearts and reflect on what is good and what is bad. This will lead them to love their neighbour.

When speaking of love, Mother is at her best and most convincing, because by definition, God is love. The pages of this book are replete with instances of deep love and indicate ways and means of practising love wherever we are and thus know the joy of giving, of sharing, of loving.

Mother Teresa speaks as the conscience of the world. She is a lighthouse for believers, sending rays of light that show the way in semi-darkness. And to non-believers in God, she is an anchor steadying their ship in rough waters.

Once, walking in New Delhi at a World Book Fair, I saw a smartly dressed Indian lady come out of a bookshop holding *We Do it for Jesus* in her hand. I went to her and said, 'Excuse me, madam, I am the author of the book you have just purchased. I would like to know what made you buy it.' The lady answered, 'I am a professor of Sciences at the Jawaharlal Nehru University in Delhi. I am an unbeliever, but I feel I need an anchor. Mother Teresa is an anchor.' Yes, Mother helps people to believe in goodness and love.

To put the reader in the proper mood for savouring a small portion of this book daily, I find no better way than to let Mother speak for herself.

At Prem Dan, which means the Gift of Love, the property given by a multinational to the Missionaries of Charity, that houses several hundred poor people, there was a driver known and feared for his speed. One evening when he was driving Mother Teresa back to Mother House, as he was truly at his best, that is, at his most dangerous for the passenger, Mother told him gently, 'See, I am not afraid to go and meet my Maker. But remember this : there is only one Mother Teresa.'

Calcutta   *E. Le Joly S.J.*
11 March 1996

January

Keep the joy of loving God
in your heart
and share this joy
with all you meet
especially your family.
Be holy — let us pray.

*L*ord give me this seeing faith,
then my work will never be
monotonous. I will find joy in
humouring the fancies and
gratifying the wishes of all poor
sufferers. O beloved sick,
how doubly dear you are to me,
when you personify Christ;
and what a privilege is mine
to be allowed to tend you.

*I*t is not enough for us to say :
'I love God.'
I also have to love my neighbour.
In the Scriptures, St. John says that
you are a liar if you say you love
God and you do not love your
neighbour. How can you love God
whom you do not see, if you do
not love your neighbour
whom you see, whom you touch,
with whom you live?
And he uses a very big word.
'You are a liar.'
It is one of those words that is
frightening to read,
and yet it is really true.

*I*t is very important for us
to realize that love, to be true,
has to hurt. I must be willing to
give whatever it takes not to harm
other people and, in fact, to do
good to them. This requires that
I be willing to give until it hurts.
Otherwise there is no true love
in me and I bring injustice,
not peace, to those around me.

*C*harity begins today.
Today somebody is suffering,
today somebody is in the street,
today somebody is hungry.
Our work is for today, yesterday
has gone, tomorrow has
not yet come.
We have only today to make
Jesus known, loved, served,
fed, clothed, sheltered.
Do not wait for tomorrow.
Tomorrow we will not have them
if we do not feed them today.

*S*ometime ago a woman came
with her child to me and said :
'Mother, I went to two or three
places to beg for food, for we
have not eaten for three days
but they told me that
I was young and I should work
and earn my living.
No one gave me anything.'
I went to get some food
for her and by the time
I returned, the baby in her arms
had died of hunger.

*E*verything starts from prayer.
Without asking God for love,
we cannot possess love and still
less are we able to give it to others.
Just as people today are speaking
so much about the poor but they
do not know or talk to the poor,
we too cannot talk so much
about prayer and yet not
know how to pray.

*H*ow do we learn to pray?
When Jesus was asked by His
disciples how to pray, He did not
teach them any methods or
techniques. He said that we should
speak to God as to our Father,
a loving Father.
Let us say this prayer
and live it :
Our Father who art in heaven
Hallowed be thy name
Thy kingdom come
Thy will be done on earth
as it is in heaven.
Give us this day our daily bread
And forgive us our trespasses
As we forgive them that trespass
against us
And lead us not into temptation
But deliver us from evil.

*I*t is simple yet so beautiful.
Is this prayer fitting me?
Can I say this prayer with
an open heart, with a clean heart?
Everything is there:
God, myself, my neighbour.
If I forgive them I can pray. There
are no complications and yet we
complicate our lives so much,
by so many additions.

*T*o students : I pray that all those
young people who have graduated,
do not carry just a piece of
paper with them but that they
carry with them love, peace and
joy. That they become the
sunshine of God's love to our
people, the hope of eternal
happiness and the burning flame
of love wherever they go. That they
become carriers of God's love.
That they be able to give what
they have received.
For they have received not to keep
but to share.

*H*ave a deep compassion
for people. To be able to have a
heart full of compassion we need
to pray. Especially be kind,
be loving to the poor. We think
we do so much for the poor,
but it is they who make us rich.
We are in debt to them.
Do you want to do something
beautiful for God?
There is a person who needs you.
This is your chance.

*T*ry to put in the hearts
of your children a love for home.
Make them long to be with
their families. So much sin
could be avoided if our people
really loved their homes.

I believe God loves the world
through us —
through you and through me.
We use Mother Teresa's name;
it is only a name, but we are real
co-workers and carriers of His love.
Today God loves the world through
us. Especially in times like these
when people are trying to
make God 'was', it is you and I,
by our love, by the purity of our
lives, by our compassion, who
prove to the world
that God 'is'.

*L*et us not be afraid to
be humble, small, helpless to
prove our love for God.
The cup of water you give the sick,
the way you lift a dying man,
the way you feed a baby,
the way you teach a dull child,
the way you give medicine to a
sufferer of leprosy,
the joy with which you smile at
your own at home — all this is
God's love in the world today.

*I*n Minneapolis, a woman in a
wheelchair, suffering continuous
convulsions from cerebral palsy
asked me what people
like her could do for others.
I told her :
You can do the most. You can do
more than any of us
because your suffering is united
with the suffering of Christ on the
Cross and it brings strength
to all of us.
There is a tremendous strength
that is growing in the world
through this continual sharing,
praying together, suffering together
and working together.

There are sick and crippled people who cannot do anything to share in the work. So they adopt a Sister or a Brother, who then involves the sick co-worker fully in whatever he or she does. The two become like one person, and they call each other their second self. I have a second self in Belgium, and when I was last there, she said to me, 'I am sure you are going to have a heavy time, with all the walking and working and talking. I know this from the pain I have in my spine.' That was just before her seventeenth operation. Each time I have something special to do, it is she behind me that gives me all the strength and courage to do it.

God dwells in us.
It doesn't matter where you are as
long as you are clean of heart.
Clean of heart means openness,
that complete freedom,
that detachment that allows you to
love God without hindrance,
without obstacles. When sin comes
into our lives that is a personal
obstacle between us and God.
Sin is nothing but slavery.

*T*o doctors : Have you experienced
the joy of loving?
You can do that as doctors.
You have a beautiful opportunity
when the sick come to you with
great trust and confidence
not only to receive a few tablets
from you but to receive your
tender love and care and especially
when you have to make a sacrifice
to look after the poor.
Jesus said :
'Whatever you do to the least of
my brethren, you do it to me.'

*T*here is much suffering in the
world — physical, material, mental.
The suffering of some can be
blamed on the greed of others.
The material and physical
suffering is suffering from hunger,
from homelessness,
from all kinds of diseases.
But the greatest suffering is being
lonely, feeling unloved,
having no one.
I have come more and more to
realize that it is being unwanted
that is the worst disease that any
human being can ever experience.

*T*o teachers : Do not neglect the
weaker children. Consider the
problems of the slow-witted,
the dropouts — what will they
become in society, if you
do not look after them?
Among the poor we have
the rich poor — children who are
better gifted.
The rich poor child can still have a
place but it is the child who is
so dull, stupid, hungry
that I must work for.

*L*et us beg from our Lady
to make our hearts 'meek and
humble' like her Son's was.
We learn humility through accepting
humiliations cheerfully.
Do not let a chance pass you by.
It is so easy to be proud, harsh,
moody and selfish, but
we have been created for greater
things. Why stoop down to things
that will spoil the
beauty of our hearts?

Nowadays, young people
especially, want to see.
You speak of love,
you speak of prayer. They want to
know how you love and
how you pray, and what
compassion means to you.
That is how they judge.
How you really live the life of a
co-worker, a carrier of God's love.

*H*umility always radiates the
greatness and glory of God.
Through humility we grow in love.
Humility is the
beginning of sanctity.

*D*on't neglect your family.
Be at home. If today so many
young people are misled,
it is because the grandparents are
in some institution, mother is so
busy that she is not there when the
child comes home from school.
There is nobody to receive them,
or play with them and they go
back into the streets where there
are drugs and drinks and so many
other things.
It is the same everywhere.
Everything depends on how much
we love one another.

*P*lease don't kill the child.
I want the child.
I am willing to accept any child
who would be aborted and give
him or her to a married couple
who will love the child and be
loved by the child. At our children's
home in Calcutta alone, we have
saved over 3,000 children from
abortion. These children have
brought such love and joy to their
adoptive parents and have grown
up so full of love and joy.

*W*hen we have nothing to give,
let us give Him that nothingness.
Let us all remain as empty as
possible, so that God can fill us.
Even God cannot fill
what is already full.
God won't force Himself on us.
You are filling the world
with the love
God has given you.

The very fact that God has placed
a certain soul in our way
is a sign that God wants us to do
something for him or her.
It is not chance;
it has been planned by God.
We are bound by conscience to
help him or her.

*W*e have small 'listening groups'
of co-workers who go to the homes
of old people and sit down with
them and let them talk.
Very old people love to have
somebody listen to them
and let them talk,
even if they have to tell
the story of thirty years ago.
To listen, when nobody else wants
to listen, is a very beautiful thing

*I*t is easy to smile at people
outside your own home.
It is so easy to take
care of the people that you
don't know well.
It is difficult to be thoughtful
and kind and to smile
and be loving to your own in the
house day after day, especially
when we are tired and in a bad
temper or bad mood.
We all have these moments and
that is the time
that Christ comes to us in a
distressing disguise.

*T*rue love always has to hurt.
It must be painful to love someone,
painful to leave someone.
You might have to die for them.
When people marry they give up
everything to love each other.
The mother who gives birth
to her child suffers much.
Only then can we truly love.
The word 'love' is so misunderstood
and so misused.

*E*ach one must do as he
has made up his mind,
not reluctantly or under
compulsion, for God loves a
cheerful giver. He gives most who
gives with joy. If in your work you
have difficulties accept them with
joy, with a big smile. The best way
to show your gratitude to God
and people is to accept
everything with joy.

February

*G*od loves you.
Love one another as He loves you.
Love is sharing,
love is giving the best we have.
We are carriers of God's love
and whoever you are,
you can become one also.

*L*ove cannot remain by itself —
it has no meaning.
Love has to be put into action
and that action is service.
A mission of love can come
only from union with God.
From that union,
love for the family,
love for one's neighbour,
love for the poor
is the natural fruit.

You can pray while you work.
Work doesn't stop prayer
and prayer doesn't stop work.
It requires only that small raising of
the mind to Him :
I love you God
I trust you
I believe in you
I need you now.
Small things like that.
They are wonderful prayers.

*T*o doctors : I have a special love
for doctors. Yours is not only a
profession but a vocation — the
vocation to be God's love,
God's compassion, God's healing
power to the suffering.
God has chosen you for a special
mission. Being a doctor means
going out and touching God
in each of the suffering, whether
it be the rich or the poor,
for sickness strikes all.

*T*here was the man we picked up
from the drain, half eaten by
worms and, after we had brought
him to the Home for the Dying
in Kalighat, he only said,
'I have lived like an animal in the
street, but I am going to die as an
angel, loved and cared for.'
Then, after we removed all the
worms from his body, all he said,
with a big smile, was :
'Sister, I'm going home to God,'
and he died. It was so wonderful
to see the greatness of a man
who could speak like that
without blaming anybody,
without comparing anything.
This is the greatness of people
who are spiritually rich even
when they are materially poor.

A cheerful giver is a great giver.
Cheerfulness is a sign of a
generous, mortified person,
who forgetting all things, even
herself, tries to please her God
in all she does.
It is often a cloak which hides
a life of sacrifice,
a continual union with God.

*D*o we believe that God's love
is infinitely more powerful,
His mercy more tender
than the evil of sin,
than all the hatred,
conflicts and tensions
that are dividing the world?
Than the most powerful bombs
and guns ever made by
human hands and minds?

*O*nce you know you have hurt
someone be the first to say sorry.
We cannot forgive unless we
know that we need forgiveness,
and forgiveness is the
beginning of love.

I once picked up a woman from a
garbage dump and she was burning
with fever; she was in her last days
and her only lament was :
'My son did this to me.'
I begged her :
You must forgive your son. In a
moment of madness, when he was
not himself, he did a thing he
regrets. Be a mother to him,
forgive him.
It took me a long time to make
her say :
'I forgive my son.'
Just before she died in my arms,
she was able to say that with a real
forgiveness. She was not concerned
that she was dying. The breaking of
the heart was that her son did not
want her. This is something you
and I can understand.

The quickest and the surest way
towards thoughtfulness is the
tongue — use it for the good
of others. If you think well of
others, you will also speak well of
others. Violence of the tongue is
very real — sharper than any knife,
wounding and creating bitterness
that only the grace of God
can heal.

*E*very day I have to sign so
many letters and sometimes I am
very tired. So I have made a
contract with Jesus :
'God bless you.
Mother Teresa MC'
are twenty-five letters, so I offer
twenty-five acts of love for that
person to whom the letter is
addressed.

*F*or parents : Vast regions of the
world are covered by spiritual
deserts. There you will find
young people marked by human
abandonment, the result of
broken relationships which affect
them to their very depths.
Even when they are thirsting for
a spiritual life, many of the young
are afflicted by doubt.
They are unable to place their
confidence in God,
to believe, since they have not
found confidence in those to whom
life had entrusted them. Separations
have wounded the innocence of
their childhood or adolescence.
The consequences are scepticism
and discouragement. What's the use
of living? Does life still have
any meaning?

I take the Lord at His word.

Faith is a gift of God.

Without it there would be no life.

And our work, to be fruitful and

beautiful, has to be built on faith.

Love and faith go together.

They complete each other.

*I*n the face of all difficulties,
doubts and objections,
trust in Him,
He will not let you down.
If God does not grant the means,
that shows He does not want you
to do that particular work.
If He wants it done,
He will give you the means.
Therefore do not worry.

*H*oliness is the acceptance
of the will of God.
Holiness is not a luxury of the few.
It is not meant for
some people only.
It is meant for you and for me.
It is a simple duty.
Because you learn to love,
you learn to be holy,
and to be able to love,
you must pray.
My progress in holiness
depends on God and myself.

*P*eople today are hungry for love,
which is the only answer to
loneliness and great poverty.
In some countries there is no
hunger for bread. But people are
suffering from terrible loneliness,
terrible despair, terrible hatred,
feeling unwanted, helpless, hopeless.
They have forgotten how to smile,
they have forgotten the beauty
of the human touch. They are
forgetting what is human love.
They need someone who will
understand and respect them.

*D*on't search for Jesus in far
lands — He is not there.
He is close to you.
He is with you.
Just keep the lamp burning
and you will always see Him.
Keep on filling the lamp
with all these little drops of love,
and you will see how sweet
is the Lord you love.

*G*od is purity Himself;
nothing impure can come before
Him. I don't think God can hate,
because God is love and
He loves us inspite of our
misery and sinfulness.
He is a loving Father and we have
only to turn to Him.
God cannot hate;
God loves because He is love,
but impurity is an obstacle
to seeing God.

*I*n Calcutta, there are visible homes
for the dying. In other countries,
many of the young are
in homes for the dying
which are invisible,
but none the less real.
Speaking of the parable
of the prodigal son,
a boy in New York told me,
'In my family it is not the son who
left us — it's the father.'
There are parents who, although
they take·care of material needs,
are in fact totally absent in the eyes
of their children.

*O*nce a beggar came to me and
said : 'Everybody is giving you
something. I also want to give you
something.' And he offered me
a ten-paisa coin.
If I accepted the money, he would
go hungry, but if I didn't, he would
be unhappy. I accepted it.
And I felt within me, that his gift
was greater than the Nobel Prize
because he gave all that he had.
I could see in his face
the joy of giving.

Gandhiji loved his people as God
loved him and one of the most
beautiful things that struck me
about him was his non-violence
and also his comparing the poor
with the service of love for God.
He said :
'He who serves the poor serves
God.' Gandhiji's non-violence,
I understand, is not only not using
guns and bombs. It is the love and
peace and compassion in our own
homes first. This is what spreads
non-violence outside the home,
if we have that love,
if we have that compassion for
each other. Jesus Christ said again
and again : 'Love one another
as I have loved you.'

I do not think I have any special
qualities.
I don't claim anything for the work.
It is His work. I am like a little
pencil in His hand, that is all.
He does the thinking.
He does the writing.
The pencil has nothing to do with
it. The pencil has only to be
allowed to be used.

*A*ll works of love are works
of peace. We do not need bombs
and guns to bring peace,
we need love and compassion.
But we also need that deep union
with God, prayer. We who have
been gathered here for the sake of
learning what is peace so as to
give it to others, let us learn,
let us understand that unless
we are full of God,
we cannot give that love,
we cannot give that peace
to others and we will not
have peace in the world.

*L*et us pray and try to live the
prayer for peace of St. Francis
of Assisi and make it our own :
Lord make me an instrument of
your peace,
where there is hatred,
I may bring love,
where there is wrong,
I may bring the spirit of
forgiveness;
where there is discord,
I may bring harmony;
where there is error,
I may bring truth;
where there is doubt,
I may bring faith;
where there is despair,
I may bring hope.
Where there are shadows,
I may bring light; where there is
sadness I may bring joy.

*P*rayer : Lord, grant that I may
seek rather to comfort than to be
comforted; to understand rather
than be understood; to love rather
than be loved, for it is by forgetting
self that one finds. It is by forgiving
that one is forgiven. It is by dying
that one awakens to eternal life.

Amen.

You and I have been created for greater things. We have not been created to just pass through this life without aim. And that greater aim is to live and be loved and we cannot love unless we know. Knowledge always leads to love and love to service.

*O*ne day a lady came to me
dressed in a very rich sari.
She told me :
'Mother, I want to share
in your work.'
I prayed for a moment to get the
right answer to give her
about sharing in my work.
And I told her :
'I would begin with the sari. You
start buying a cheaper sari each
month, and the money you save,
you bring it to me for the poor.'
So she started buying cheaper
saris and she said it changed her
life. She has really understood
sharing. And she told me that she
has received much more than she
has given.

*W*hen the time comes and we can't pray, it is very simple : if Jesus is in my heart let him pray, let me allow him to pray in me, to talk to his Father in the silence of my heart. If I cannot speak, he will speak for me; if I cannot pray, he will pray. That's why we say : 'Jesus in my heart, I believe in your faithful love for me.'

March

God has created us to love
and to be loved, and this is the
beginning of prayer — to know
that he loves me,
to know that
I have been created
for greater things.

$\mathcal{H}$ow do we begin that love,
that peace and hope?
The family that prays together stays
together; and if we stay together,
naturally we will love one another
and want each other. I feel today
we need to bring prayer back.
Teach your children to pray
and pray with them.

*W*hat does God say to us?
He says: 'I have called you by your
name, you are mine; water will not
drown you, fire will not burn you,
I will give up nations for you,
you are precious to me,
I love you. Even if a
mother could forget her child,
I will not forget you. I have carved
you in the palm of my hand.'
So also, the people who come in
contact with you are precious to
Him. Help them to grow in holiness
because holiness is not a luxury
reserved for a few.
It is a simple duty for you and
for me and for all.

*W*e know that if we really want
to love, we must learn to forgive.
Forgive and ask to be forgiven;
excuse rather than accuse.
Reconciliation begins first,
not with others but with ourselves.
It starts with having a clean heart
within. A clean heart is able
to see God in others.
We must radiate God's love.

*L*et anyone who comes to you
go away feeling better and happier.
Every one should see goodness in
your face, in your eyes, in your
smile. Joy shows from the eyes,
it appears when we speak and
walk. It cannot be kept closed
inside us. It reacts outside.
Joy is very infectious.

*I*t is a wonderful feeling to know
the presence of God and how He
takes care of us. Share that joy with
others and by sharing it, give life
back into the family. My prayer for
you and your country is that we
may realize the greatness of God's
love for us and with that love
protect the unborn child,
the greatest gift of God for each
of us and for the world.

*P*rayer is a joy.
Prayer is the sunshine
of God's love,
prayer is hope of eternal
happiness, prayer is the
burning flame of God's love
for you and for me.
Let us pray for each other,
for this is the best way to love
one another.

How do we learn to pray?
By praying. It is very hard to pray
if one does not know how.
We must help ourselves to learn.
Pray with absolute trust in
God's loving care for you
and let Him fill you with joy that
you may preach without preaching.

'Open your eyes and see.'
There is not just hunger
for a piece of bread,
there is hunger for
understanding love,
for the word of God.
Nakedness is not only
for a piece of cloth,
nakedness is the loss
of human dignity,
the loss of that beautiful
virtue of purity
which is so misused nowadays.

I will never forget the day I was
walking down a street in London
and saw a man sitting all alone,
looking so terribly lonely.
I walked up to him and I took
his hand and shook it.
And he exclaimed :
'Oh, after so long, this is the
first time I've felt the warmth
of a human hand.'
And then his face brightened up.
He was a different being.
He felt that there was somebody
who really wanted him,
somebody who really cared.
I never realized before that
such a small action could
bring so much joy.

*L*et us not be satisfied with just
giving money. Money is not
enough, for money one can get.
I would like more people to give
their hands to serve and their hearts
to love — to recognize the poor in
their own homes, towns and
countries and to reach out to them
in love and compassion, giving
where it is most needed, and share
the joy of loving with everyone.

*W*hen he was dying
on the Cross, Jesus said : 'I thirst.'
Jesus is thirsting for our love,
and this is the thirst of everyone,
poor and rich alike. We all thirst for
the love of others, that they go out
of their way to avoid harming us
and do good to us.
This is the meaning of true love,
to give until it hurts.

*S*omeone once asked me,
if suddenly the need for your work
among the poorest of the poor
ceased to exist, what would you do
with the rest of your life?
I answered : We would be
unemployed like so many people
who have lost their jobs.
But Jesus said :
'You will always have the
poor with you.'

We get so many visitors every day
at Mother House in Calcutta.
When I meet them I give each one
my 'business card'. On it is written :
The fruit of silence is prayer;
The fruit of prayer is faith;
The fruit of faith is love;
The fruit of love is service;
The fruit of service is peace.
This is very good 'business'! And it
makes people think. Sometimes,
they ask me to explain it. But you
see, everything begins with prayer
that is born in the silence of our
hearts. Among yourselves you can
share your own experience of your
need to pray, and how you found
prayer, and what the fruit of prayer
has been in your own lives.

*I*s my heart so clean that
I can see the face of God in my
brother, my sister who is that black
one, that white one, that naked
one, that one suffering from
leprosy, that dying one?
And this is what we must pray for.
Because God lives in us and makes
us godly, we are one another's
brothers and sisters — one big
family of God's children.

*L*et us remember
that Jesus has said :
'Whatever you do to the least of my
brothers, you do it to me.'
Just think — that little smile that
you give to a lonely person,
that hand you give a blind person
to cross the road, that little bit of
food you sacrifice for someone
who is hungry, you do it for Him.

I will never forget the experience I had in visiting a home where they kept all the old parents of sons and daughters who had put them into an institution and perhaps forgotten them. These old people had everything — good food, comfortable place, television, everything, but everyone was looking towards the door. And I did not see a single one with a smile on the face.

I turned to Sister and asked : 'Why are they not smiling?'

I am so used to seeing the smile on our people, even the dying ones smile. And Sister said : 'This is the way it is nearly every day. They are expecting, they are hoping that a son or daughter will come to visit them.' It is this neglect to love that brings spiritual poverty.

*T*he fruit of prayer
is the deepening of love,
deepening of faith.
If we believe, we will be able
to pray, and the fruit of love is
service. Therefore works of love are
always works of peace, and to be
able to put our hearts and hands
into loving service we must know
God, we must know God is love,
that He loves us and that He has
created us — each one of us —
for greater things.

*I*f you are humble
nothing will touch you.
If you are a saint, thank God.
If you are a sinner,
do not remain so.

A gentleman once asked me what
we should do to remove
poverty from India. I said :
If you want to love the poor you
must share with them.
If you want to remove poverty,
share with the poor.

God has His own ways and
means to work in the hearts of
men, and we do not know
how close they are to Him.
By their actions we will always
know whether they are
at God's disposal or not.

*W*e must not be surprised
when we hear of murders,
of killings, of wars, of hatred.
If a mother can kill
her own child,
what is left for us
to kill each other.

I don't want the work to become
a business but to remain a work
of love. I want you to have that
complete confidence that
God won't let us down. Take Him
at His word and seek first the
Kingdom of Heaven, and all else
will be added on. Joy, peace and
unity are more important than
money. If God wants me to do
something, He gives me the means.

I remember that at the beginning
of my work I had a very high fever
and in that delirious fever I went
before St. Peter. He said to me :
'Go back. There are no slums
in heaven!'
So I got very angry with him and
I said : Very well! Then I will fill
heaven with slum people and
you will have slums there.
Then you will be forced to
let me in. We will all have
to go home to God.

*I*n his passion Jesus taught us
how to forgive out of love,
how to forget out of humility.
So let us at the beginning of the
Passion of Christ examine our
hearts fully and see if there is
any unforgiven hurt,
any unforgotten bitterness.

*I*n Calcutta, we cope with 9,000
people every day and the day we
don't cook, they don't eat. One day,
a Sister came and told me :
'Mother, there is no more rice for
Friday and Saturday; we will have
to tell the people that we don't
have it.' On Friday morning at
about 9 o'clock, a truck full of
bread arrived. The Government had
closed the schools for some reason.
All the bread was brought to us
and for two days our people ate
bread, and bread and bread! I knew
why God
had closed the schools.
Those thousands of people had to
know that God loved them,
that He cared for them.

*I*f we really want to pray,
we must first learn to listen :
for in the silence of the heart
God speaks. And to be able to see
that silence, to be able to hear
God, we need a clean heart.
Let us listen to God, to what He
has to say. We cannot speak unless
we have listened, unless we have
made our connection with God.
From the fullness of the heart,
the mouth will speak,
the mind will think.

I am not the centrepiece on a
prize-giving day. It is Christ using
me as his instrument to unite
all the people present.
That is what I see happening :
people coming to meet each other
because of their need for God.
The wonderful thing about it is
that there is a religious atmosphere;
they all speak about God.
This is a great experience for me.
I feel that to bring all these people
together to talk about God
is really wonderful.
A new hope for the world.

*S*elf-knowledge puts us on
our knees, and it is very
necessary for love.
For knowledge of God gives love,
and knowledge of self
gives humility.

*T*here is no limit,
because God is love and love is God.
And so you are really
in love with God,
and God's love is infinite.
And that's why it's not
how much you do,
but how much love you put
into the action.

*B*efore God we are all poor.
We are all handicapped in one way
or another. Sometimes it can be
seen on the outside,
sometimes it is in the inside.
The healthy person may be closer
to dying or even more dead than
the person who is dying.
They might be spiritually dead,
only it does not show.

April

1 APRIL

I can't bear being photographed
but I make use of everything
for the glory of God.
When I allow a person to take a
photograph, I tell Jesus to take one
soul to Heaven out of Purgatory.

A good and necessary way
to prepare for Easter
is to turn back to God
if we have been away from Him.
God loves each one of us with
a most tender and personal love.
His longing for me is dearer
than my longing for Him.
If we are truly humble,
we will see what keeps us away
from Him, and will want to take it
away. If you want to grow in
holiness this Lent, put your hand in
Mary's, and ask her to help you to
become meek and humble.

*W*e ourselves feel that
what we are doing is just
a drop in the ocean.
But if that drop was not there,
I think the ocean would be
less by that missing drop.
We don't have to think in numbers.
We can only love
one person at a time —
serve one person at a time.

There is always the danger that we
may just do the work for the sake
of the work. It is a danger if we
forget to whom we are doing it.
This is where the respect and love
and devotion come in, that we give
it and do it to God, to Christ and
that is why we do it
as beautifully as possible.
The beautiful experience that we
have by serving, we must pass on
to people who have not had it.
It is one of the great
rewards of our work.

The future is not in our hands.
We have no power over it.
We can act only today.
We have a sentence in our
Constitution that says :
'We will allow the good God to
make plans for the future —
for yesterday has gone,
tomorrow has not yet come and
we have only today to make Him
known, loved and served.'
So we do not worry about
the future.

*O*nce we had no sugar for our
children. I don't know how, but a
little child heard that Mother Teresa
needed sugar. He went home
and he told his parents :
'I will not eat sugar for three days.
I will give my sugar to
Mother Teresa.' After three days,
the parents brought the child to our
house. In his hand, he had a little
bottle of sugar. He could scarcely
pronounce my name but he taught
me that it is not how much
we give but how much love
we put in the giving.

*W*e have absolutely no difficulty regarding having to work in countries with many faiths. We treat all people as children of God. They are our brothers and sisters. We show great respect to them. Our work is to encourage these people, Christians as well as non-Christians, to do works of love. Every work of love done with a full heart brings people closer to God.

*A*t the Home for the Dying
in Kalighat, a visitor wondered at
the peace that pervaded
everywhere. I said simply :
God is here.
Castes and creeds mean nothing.
It does not matter that they are not
of my faith.

I see Christ in every person
I touch because He said :
'I was hungry, I was thirsty,
I was naked, I was sick,
I was suffering, I was homeless
and you took care of me.'

*H*omelessness is not only of
bricks but homelessness comes from
that terrible loneliness that the
unwanted, the unloved know along
their way. Are we there?
Do we know them?
Do we see them?

*T*o the cast of a musical
performance in Calcutta,
I said : Your work and our work
complete each other.
What we are doing is needed in the
world as never before.
You are giving them joy
by your action and we are doing
the same by service.
And it is the same action
whether you are singing
and dancing and we are
rubbing and scrubbing.
You are filling
the world with the love
God has given you.

I'll never forget my own mother. She used to be very busy the whole day, but as soon as the evening came, she used to move very fast to get ready to meet my father. At that time, we didn't understand, we used to smile, we used to laugh and we used to tease her. But now I remember what a tremendous, delicate love she had for him. It didn't matter what happened, she was ready there with a smile to meet him. Today we have no time. The father and the mother are so busy. The children come home and there's no one to love them, to smile at them. That's why I'm very strict with my co-workers. I always say : Family first. If you are not there, how will your love grow for one another?

*B*e the living expression
of God's kindness;
kindness in your eyes,
kindness in your face,
kindness in your smile,
kindness in your warm greetings.
We are all but His instruments
who do our little bit and pass by.
I believe that the way in which
an act of kindness is done is
as important as the action itself.

*I*f sometimes people have had to
die of starvation, it is not because
God didn't care for them,
but because you and I were not
instruments of love in the hands of
God, to give them bread,
because we did not recognize Him,
when once more the hungry Christ
came in distressing disguise.

*E*ven if my mouth is closed,
with my eyes I can talk to you for
a whole half hour. Looking at your
eyes I can tell whether there is
peace in your heart or not.
We see people radiating joy,
and in their eyes you can see
purity. If we want our minds to
have silence, keep a silence
of the eyes. Use your two eyes to
help you to pray better.

*P*ray with me :
Make us worthy, Lord, to serve
our fellow men throughout
the world who live and die in
poverty and hunger.
Give them through our hands
their daily bread
and by our understanding love
give peace and joy.

*P*eople throughout the world may
look different or have a different
religion, education or position,
but they are all the same.
They are the people to be loved.
They are all hungry for love.
The people you see in the streets
of Calcutta are hungry in body,
but the people in London or
New York also have a hunger
which must be satisfied.
Every person needs to be loved.

*I*n the Scriptures, it is written,
'I looked for one to comfort me
and I found none.'
Jesus is your child, your spouse,
your neighbour, looking for
someone to comfort Him.
Are you there?
Let us make a resolution :
I will be there for my child,
my spouse, my neighbour — not just
in words, but by my sharing and
sacrificing. Maybe just a beautiful
smile instead of that ugly look,
maybe a beautiful word instead
of that angry word. Let us take
the trouble to be that one
to comfort him.

We are grateful for the thousands
of opportunities Jesus gives us to
bring hope into a multitude of lives.
By our concern for the individual
sufferer we will help
our troubled world at the brink
of despair, to discover a new
reason to live or to die with a smile
of contentment on its lips,
for at the end of life
we go home to Jesus.

You cannot love two persons
perfectly. But you can love all
men perfectly if you love the
one God in them all.
One should centre his mind
and heart, his life and activity
on God and see him in every
human sufferer.

Once a man came to the Home
for the Dying in Kalighat and he
just walked right into the ward.
I was there. After a while he came
back and said to me :
'I came here with so much hate in
my heart, hate for God and hate for
man. I came here empty, faithless,
embittered and I saw a Sister inside
giving her wholehearted attention
to that patient there and I realized
that God still lives. Now I go out
a different man. I believe there
is a God and He loves us still.'
I want this to be imprinted on your
mind that God loves the world
through you and through me today.

*L*et us be very sincere in our
dealings with each other,
and have the courage to accept
each other as we are.
Do not be surprised or become
preoccupied at each other's
failures — rather, see and find in
each other the good,
for each one of us is created
in the image of God.

*Y*oung people today aim at one
thing only, to give all or nothing.
And this is one of the reasons why
I have accepted to come here
because I hope that all people,
the young men and women who
will be involved in Gandhiji's work,
will dedicate their lives
to spread the gift of God that was
given to Gandhiji —
that love for his people,
love for non-violence.

I love all religions but I am
in love with my own.
If people become better Hindus,
better Muslims, better Buddhists
by our acts of love, then there is
something else growing there.
They come closer
and closer to God.
When they come closer,
they have to choose.

*Y*ou will find Calcutta all over the
world if you have eyes to see.
The streets of Calcutta
lead to every man's door.
I know that you may want to make
a trip to Calcutta, but it is
easy to love people far away.
It is not always easy to love those
people who live beside us.
What about the ones I dislike
or look down upon?

*T*he woman is the heart
of the home.
Let us pray that we women realize
the reason of our existence :
to love and be loved and
through this love become
instruments of peace in the world.

*W*hen I received the news of the
Nobel Peace Prize,
I said :
I am myself unworthy of the prize.
I thank God for making the world
acknowledge the existence of the
poor and the works of love
to be works of peace.
On the same day, a tiny abandoned
infant was brought to Shishu
Bhavan (children's home) in
Calcutta and was named
Shanti (Peace).
The infant survived.

*H*oliness is not something
extraordinary, not something for
only a few with brains, with
intellectual powers that can reason,
that can discuss, that can have long
talks and read very wonderful
books. Holiness is for every one of
us as a simple duty — the
acceptance
of God with a smile, at all times,
anywhere and everywhere.

*W*e can never know how much
good a simple smile can do.

*I*t is so beautiful that we complete
each other! What we are doing in
the slums, maybe you cannot do.
What you are doing at the level
where you are called — in your
family life, in your college life,
in your work — we cannot do.
But together you and we are
doing something beautiful for God.

May

*P*eople who love each other
fully and truly are the happiest
people in the world.
They may have little, they
may have nothing but they
are happy people.
Everything depends on how
we love one another.

I appeal to you, young people —
you the hope of our country,
you the joy of our country,
bring that joy with peace in our
homes, in our country,
and we will be
able to be the sunshine of
God's love in the whole world.

I am sure that all people know
deep down inside that the little
child in the mother's womb is a
human being from the moment of
conception, created in the image of
God to love and to be loved.
Let us pray that nobody will be
afraid to protect that little child,
to help that little child to be born.
Jesus said : 'If you receive a little
child in my name, you receive me.'

*P*ray at home for only
five minutes.
Prayer is simply talking to God.
He speaks to us, we listen.
We speak to Him, He listens.
A two-way process :
speaking and listening.

*W*hat do we ask?
'Give us this day our daily bread.'
What is our daily bread?
It is peace and love.
Besides the bread for our bodies,
we need that other bread for our
souls to be able to live.
For man does not live on bread
alone. And each of us before we
pass the prayer on to somebody
else, let us put that prayer into life.
Let us spread the good news that
prayer is our strength.

*W*e must acknowledge the dignity
of the poor, respect them, esteem
them, love them, serve them.
Often I think they are the ones
to whom we owe our greatest
gratitude. They teach us by
their faith, their resignation,
their patience in suffering.
They allow us to help them.
We should experience not pity but
compassion towards the poor.

I feel Indian to the most profound
depths of my soul.
The Missionaries of Charity
share in their way of dressing,
the way of life of the poorest in
this world. Of course India needs
technicians, skilled men, economists,
doctors, nurses for her development.
She needs plans and a general
co-ordinated action. Meanwhile
people have to live,
they have to be given food to eat,
be taken care of and dressed. Our
field of work is the present India.
While these needs continue,
our work will continue.

*F*or me, life is the most beautiful
gift of God to mankind,
therefore people and nations who
destroy life by abortion and
euthanasia are the poorest.
I do not say legal or illegal,
but I think that no human hand
should be raised to kill life,
since life is God's life in us,
even in an unborn child.

I could not help but examine my
conscience before her.
And I asked :
What would I say if I was
in her place?
And my answer was very simple.
I would have tried to draw a
little attention to myself.
I would have said :
I am hungry, I am dying, I am
cold, I am in pain, or something.
She gave me much more than I
gave her. This is the greatest love.

It is one thing to say I am a
sinner, but let someone else say
that about me and then I feel it —
I am up in arms. If I am
falsely accused I may suffer,
whereas if correction be founded on
even a small reality — something in
me having deserved it —
then often it hurts more.
We must be happy that our faults
are known as they are.

*R*iches can suffocate if
they are not used in the
right way, whether they are
spiritual riches or material.

A gentleman once came to me
and said that he wanted to give a
big donation. After giving the
donation, he said,
'That is something outside
of me, but I want to give
something of me.'
So he comes regularly to the
Home for the Dying at Kalighat and
talks to the people there who are
sick and dying, helps them to
bathe and shave.
He wanted to give
something of himself and now
he is giving it.

*T*o women : You and I, being
women, we have this tremendous
thing in us, understanding love.
I see that so beautifully in our
people, in our poor women,
who day after day, meet suffering,
accept suffering for the
sake of their children.
I have seen mothers going without
so many things,
even resorting to begging,
so that the children may have
what they need.

I think it is very important for us
as co-workers to put that
understanding love into action.
A co-worker is not a name only.
A co-worker is not first belonging
to something. Any person who
carries that love, who shares that
love is a co-worker in action.
And so let us come to this simple
definition of a co-worker :
A co-worker is a person who puts
her love for God into living action
and service to the poor.
Where? In the family first and then
for others. We must not neglect our
homes and go out before we have
started inside and begin with
ourselves first. Then, because we
have practiced that, we are able to
give to others.

*F*or us to be able to love
we need to see,
we need to touch,
and that is why we read in the
Scriptures, Jesus made the poor
the hope of salvation for
you and for me.

*E*ven though I cannot personally meet and talk to each one of you, you are in my daily prayer. My deep gratitude to you for all the ways in which you help us by serving the poor alongside us, and for all your prayers and sacrifices. Your sufferings accepted in love by Jesus are the source of many graces. You are sharing wholeheartedly in all we do.

*W*hereas you work to bring
about peace, why is it you do not
work, they ask, to lessen war? If
you are working for peace, that
peace lessens war. But I won't mix
in politics. War is the fruit of
politics, and so I don't involve
myself,
that's all. If I get stuck in politics,
I will stop loving. Because I will
have to stand by one, and not by
all. This is the difference.

*G*ive a person tender love and
care. Your radiating concern,
your radiating joy will give that
person great hope.

*B*ecome holy. Each one of us has
a capacity to become holy and
the way to holiness is prayer.

*L*ove begins at home;
love lives in homes, and that is
why there is so much suffering
and so much unhappiness
in the world today. If we listen to
Jesus, He will tell us
what He said before :
'Love one another, as I have loved
you.' He has loved us through
suffering, dying on the Cross for us,
and so if we are to love one
another, if we are to bring
that love into life again, we have to
begin at home.

*E*very human being comes from
God. We all know what is
the love of God for us.
Whatever we believe, we know that
if we really want to love,
we must learn to forgive.
We must radiate God's love.

*W*hen I was invited to China,
I was asked, 'What is a communist
to you?' And I said : A child of
God, my brother and my sister.
And nobody had another word
to say. There was perfect silence.
And it is true, because the same
loving hand created you,
created me, created the man
on the street.

*L*et us ask our Lady, in a very
special way :
Mary, mother of Jesus,
be a mother to each of us, that we,
like you, may be pure in heart,
that we, like you, love Jesus;
that we, like you, serve the poorest
for we are all poor.
First let us love our neighbours and
so fulfill God's desire
that we become carriers of His
love and compassion.

I can give you nothing,
I have nothing to give — but what I
want from you is that when we
look together and we see the poor
in our own family, we begin
at home to love until it hurts.
If we know our own people we
will know then who is our next
door neighbour. Do we know the
people around us? In one of the
houses the Sisters visited,
a woman living alone had been
dead for many days
before she was found and the
people around her did not even
know her name.

The same is true for our
sufferers of leprosy,
the same for our crippled,
for our unloved,
for our uncared.
It is the same thing;
they need love,
they need compassion,
they need a human touch.
Touch the sufferer of leprosy
with your kindness.

*T*o students of medicine :
I beg of you not to add to the
millions of doctors already present
who are just doling out medicines.
You must treat each patient with
love and compassion and fulfill all
the hopes they come with.
Your hands are instruments
of peace and are used to restore
life while at the same time others
use them to cause destruction.
Peace in the world is brought
about not by force but by love.

*M*y prayer for you will be that
you may grow in the likeness of
Christ through your kindness,
through your compassion and
through your healing power that
God has entrusted to you.
And you pray for us that we may
keep doing God's work with great
love, that we don't spoil His work.

*T*hou shalt love the Lord
thy God with thy whole heart,
with thy whole soul
and with all thy mind.
This is the command of our
great God, and He cannot
command the impossible.

*T*ake away your eyes from yourself
and rejoice that you have
nothing — that you are nothing —
that you can do nothing. Give Jesus
a big smile each time your
nothingness frightens you.
Just keep the joy of Jesus as
your strength — be happy and
at peace, accept whatever
He takes with a big smile.

June

I think the world today is upside down. Everybody seems to be in such a terrible rush, anxious for greater development and greater riches and so on. There is much suffering because there is so very little love in homes and in family life. We have no time for our children, we have no time for each other; there is no time to enjoy each other. In the home begins the disruption of the peace of the world.

*S*tart by making your own home
a place where peace, happiness and
love abound, through your love for
each member of your family and
for your neighbour.

*W*hat a shame if one of our brothers or sisters dies of hunger because of our neglect and selfishness. We will never feel what the poor feel, because we do not have to worry about our next meal, about our clothes, our comforts, we have them all in abundance. Love means to share with others.

*H*ow can we stress respect for life — from the womb to those who are dying on the streets? We must realize the greatness of life. Every child is a gift from God. I think it is important to realize that we have been created for greater things — to love and be loved. When we destroy love, then who will be there for us? Every single person, young and old, must realize this. When we realize this, then we will be able to share that love.

We will be able to accept each other. We will be really free and able for Jesus.

*Y*oung people, make a strong resolution today, that we will keep our purity pure, our chastity chaste, our virginity virgin! The greatest gift you can give to each other on the day of your wedding, or to God, on the day when you join the priesthood or religious life, is a pure heart, a pure body.

*W*hen we say no to violence, we always imagine a knife, a bomb, a gun. However, to me, violence is caused by our attitude. For example, telling people that they are good for nothing, that they are lazy, and that they are this, and that they are that. I think this a great violence. If you and I could only make that one strong resolution that we will say 'no' to violence, and say 'yes' to peace by our kindness, by our attitude towards each other, even in a small thing — a smile when we meet each other, it would help more than anything.

*L*ove does not live on words nor
can it be explained by words —
especially the love which serves
God. Simple acts of love and care
keep the light of God burning.

*J*oy is love, the normal result of a
heart burning with love.
Joy is a need and a physical power.
Our lamp will be burning with
sacrifices made out of love if we
have joy.

*H*ow can we help students to see
the richness of community service?
Teach them. And ask them to love
in their own family. Love begins at
home. Lots of love always brings
lots of peace. That's why it is
important for the family to pray
together, and they will stay together
and love one another. Then it will
be easier to be a fountain of love
for each other.

*I*f I was told, you may only stay
here and work for the poor if you
give up your faith, your religion,
which would I choose? My religion
nobody can take from me, and
therefore they cannot refuse it, they
cannot take it from me. This is
something within me. If there is no
alternative and if that is the only
way that Christ wants to come
amongst these people by
radiating His life, His love for them
through my actions and so draw
them to Him,
I would stay to serve them.
I wouldn't give up . . . I would be
ready to give my life,
but not my faith.

*O*ur work should not be
superficial but deep. We must reach
the heart.
To reach the heart we must do —
love is proved in deeds.
People are attracted more by what
they see than by what they hear.
If people wish to help,
let them come and see —
the reality is more attractive than
the abstract idea.

*H*ave you ever gone to help any
charitable organization in your own
country? If you have never gone,
I think you should not miss such
an opportunity in life. It gives you
the experience of sheer joy and
fulfilment. You will get in touch
with Christ as you would
nowhere else.

*N*one of us, I am sure knows what is the pain of hunger, but one day I learned it from a little child. I found the child in the street and I saw in her face that terrible hunger that I have seen in many eyes. Without questioning her I gave her a piece of bread, and then I saw that the little child was eating the bread crumb by crumb. And I said to her : Eat the bread. And that little one looked at me and said : 'I am afraid because when the bread is finished I will be hungry again.'

The essential thing is not what
we say, but what God says to us
and through us. All our words
will be useless unless they
come from within.
Why not try and hold your tongue?
You know what you can do but
you do not know how much
the other can bear.

*O*vercome the finite with the
infinite. Christ has created you
because He wanted you.
I know what you feel —
terrible longing, with dark
emptiness — and yet, He is the one
in love with you. I do not know if
you have seen these few lines
before, but they fill and empty me :
'My God, my God, what is a heart
That thou should'st so eye
and woo,
Pouring upon it all thy heart
As if thou hadst nothing else
to do . . . ?'

*I*n Yemen, which is entirely a
Muslim country, I asked one of the
rich people to build a Masjid there.
People needed a place to pray,
I said to him. They are all
Muslim brothers and sisters.
They need to have a place where
they can meet God.

*D*ear God, when it comes to helping those in need, help me to see more than myself. I don't think there is anyone who needs God's grace and help more than I do. I feel so forsaken and confused at times. And I think that is exactly why God uses me, because I cannot claim any credit for what gets done. On the contrary I need His help twenty-four hours a day.

*E*verything starts with prayer.
Love to pray — feel the need to
pray often during the day and take
the trouble to pray. If you want to
pray better, you must pray more.
The more you pray
the easier it becomes.
Perfect prayer does not consist
of many words but in the
fervour of the desire which
raises the heart to Jesus.

*O*ften you see small and big
wires, new and old, cheap and
expensive electric cables that are
useless, for until the current passes
through them there will be no light.
The wires are you and me, the
current is God. We have the power
to let the current pass through us —
to use us — or refuse to be used
and allow darkness to spread.

It is easy to love people far away,
very easy to think of the hungry
people in India.
You must see first that there is
love at home and at your next-door
neighbour's and in the street you
live in, in the town you live in
and only then outside.

*I*f we are full of sin,
God cannot fill us, because even
God himself cannot fill what is full.
That's why we need forgiveness
to become empty, and then
God fills us with Himself.

*W*e must not drift away from the
humble works, because these are
the works nobody will do. They are
never too small. We are so small
we look at things in a small way.
Even if we do a small thing for
somebody, God, being almighty,
sees everything as great.
For there are many people who can
do big things. But there
are very few people who
will do the small things.

Charity for the poor is like a living
flame; the drier the fuel, the
brighter it burns. In your service to
the poor do not give only your
hands but also your hearts.
Charity to be fruitful must cost us.
Give until it hurts. To love, it is
necessary to give : to give
it is necessary to be free
from selfishness.

I will remember always the last
time I visited Venezuela in South
America. A rich family had given
the Sisters land to build a children's
home, so I went to thank them.
And there in the family I found
their eldest child was terribly
disabled. And I asked the mother :
What is the child's name?
The mother answered : 'Professor of
Love, because this child is teaching
us the whole time how to express
love in action.'
There was a beautiful smile
on the mother's face.
'Professor of Love' they called their
child, so terribly disabled,
so disfigured!

I don't want that you give from your abundance. I want you to understand through direct contact. The poor need deeds, not words. It is not my task to evaluate existing systems, economic, social, or political structures and ideologies. Everyone has a conscience and must follow it.

I do not agree with the big way of
doing things. To us, what matters is
an individual. To get to love a
person, we must come in close
contact with him. If we wait till we
get numbers, then we will be
lost in the numbers, and we will
never be able to show that love
and respect for the person.
I believe in person-to-person;
every person is Christ for me, and
since there is only one Jesus,
that person is the one person in the
world at that moment.

*S*anctity is not a luxury for the
few. It is a simple duty for you
and me. I have to be a saint in
my way and you in yours.
Thoughtfulness is the beginning
of great sanctity. If you learn
this art of being thoughtful
you will become
more and more like Christ, for
His heart was meek and
He always thought of others.

*W*e need to find God and God
cannot be found in noise
and restlessness. God is the
friend of silence.
See how nature — trees and flowers
and grass — grow in silence.
See the stars, the moon and
the sun, how they move in silence.
The more we receive in silent
prayer, the more we can give
in our active life.

We have to realize that to
be forgiven, we have to be
able to forgive.
If only the people in Northern
Ireland and in other places could
learn to forgive, I think peace
would come to them.

*T*his sharing of love in His poor
has brought us all so close to each
other and so, closer to the poor;
and by doing so we have come to
know the poor.

This knowledge has led us to love
and sacrifice, to personal service for
our neighbour.

Therefore I appeal to every one of
you, rich, young or old, to give
your own hands to serve Christ in
the poor and your hearts to love
Him in them.

July

*M*ake every effort to walk
in the presence of God. To see
God in everyone you must live
your morning meditation
throughout the day.
Smile at one another.
It is not always easy.
Sometimes we find it hard to smile
at somebody, then we pray.

*E*ven if you write a letter for a
blind man, or you just sit and
listen to someone, or you take the
mail for him, or you visit somebody
or bring a flower to somebody, or
wash clothes for somebody or clean
the house — small things,
but God sees everything great.

My aim is to bring people closer
to God through the work of charity.
The soul alone faces God's gift of
faith. It is for the soul to accept or
refuse the gift. The act of
acceptance or refusal causes
conversion. Therefore, conversion is
the work of God in the soul — and
not mine to give.

I remember my mother, my father
and the rest of us praying together
each evening. It is God's greatest
gift to the family. It maintains family
unity. So go back to family prayer
and teach your children to pray
and pray with them.
Through prayer you will find out
what God wants you to do.

*G*ive love in action. Our works of
love are nothing but works of
peace. Let us do them with greater
love and efficiency : each in his or
her own work, in daily life,
at home and with one's neighbour.
Be happy and at peace.
Accept whatever He gives and give
whatever He takes with a big smile.

*W*e must never think any one of us is indispensable. God has His ways and means. God may allow everything to go upside down in the hands of a very talented and capable person. Unless the work is interwoven with love, it is useless. God will not ask that person how many books he has read but God will ask him if he has done his best for the love of Him.

*M*aybe there is a rich person
who has no one to visit him;
he has plenty of other things,
he is nearly drowned in them,
but there is not that touch
and he needs your touch.
I was walking down the street and
a man walked up to me and said :
'Are you Mother Teresa?' And I
said : Yes. 'Please send one of your
Sisters to our house. I'm half blind
and my wife is nearly mental and
we are simply longing to hear a
human voice.' When I sent the
Sisters there they found it was true.
They had everything but no one to
call their own. Their sons and
daughters were very far from them.
They were unwanted now, unusable,
so to say, unprofitable and so
they were dying of sheer loneliness.

I think we should teach our
children to love one another at
home. They can learn this only
from their father and mother,
when they see the parents' love for
each other.

*W*hen I was crossing into Gaza,
I was asked at the checkpost
whether I was carrying
any weapons.
I replied :
Oh yes, my prayer books.

I want you to find the poor here, right in your own home first. Be that good news to your own people first. Very often we are all smiles outside, but we are all sad inside and when we come home we have no time to smile.

A woman brought a ten-week-old baby to me. The child had Down's Syndrome. Tears streamed down the mother's face as she begged me to pray that her child survive the heart operation she was about to undergo. I told her : God has given you this great gift of life. If He wants you to give the gift back to Him, give it willingly with love.

*J*oy is prayer, joy is strength,
joy is love. Joy is a net of love
by which you can catch souls.
She gives most who gives with joy.
The best way to show our gratitude
to God and the people is to
accept everything with joy.

Sometime ago, a man came to
Mother House with a prescription.
His only child was dying. He asked
me to help him to get the
medicine. Right at that moment,
a man came with a basket full of
used medicines which he had
collected. Right on top was the
medicine the man needed.
If it had been inside,
I wouldn't have seen it.
There are millions of children in the
world — see God's concern to get
the medicine for that child in the
slums of Calcutta.
That is God's tenderness and love.
That is loving trust —
Divine Providence.

*O*nce the longing for money comes, the longing also comes for what money can give — superfluous things. Our needs will increase, for one thing leads to another and the result will be endless dissatisfaction.

It is not a sin to be rich.

When it provokes avarice, it becomes a sin. Richness is given by God and it is our duty to divide it with those less favoured.

*L*et us bring that love, that compassion and share that with our people who need it. They do not need pity and sympathy but they will enrich you. My Sisters and I have been enriched with the love that we have received from our people and to us there is no difference who they are, what they are. They are all brothers and sisters and as such they are the ones to whom we belong and who belong to us because we are the children of God, created by the same loving hand of God.

*R*eligion is not something that you
or I can touch. Religion is the
worship of God — therefore a matter
of conscience. I alone must decide
for myself and you for yourself,
what we choose. For me the
religion I live and use to worship
God is the Catholic religion. For me
this is my very life, my joy and the
greatest gift of God in His love for
me. He could have given me no
greater gift.

I love my people very much, more
than myself, and so naturally I wish
to give them the joy of possessing
the treasure that is my religion, but
it is not mine to give, nor can I
force it on anyone. So also no man,
no law, no government has the
right to prevent or force me, or
anyone, if I choose to embrace the
religion that gives me peace, joy
and love.

*A*t a children's party at the
Tollygunge Club in Calcutta, when
we were celebrating the Silver
Jubilee of our Congregation, the
children were patting the luscious,
thick, green grass of the
beautiful lawns with their hands,
and they asked me what made the
blades grow so strong. They had
never seen such grass.

I saw many children who did not
eat more than one sweet out of the
packet distributed to them, in which
there were cakes, buns, sweets,
fruits, and I asked them why. They
answered me that they had brothers
and sisters at home, and they
would share with them.

I am often asked, after Mother
Teresa who?
That will be no trouble. God will
find a more humble person, more
obedient to Him, more faithful,
someone smaller with a deeper
faith, and He will do still greater
things through her.
Let the Missionaries of Charity and
the co-workers, in every country
wherever they are, meet God with
a smile — everywhere they go,
in everyone.

*L*ove to pray. Feel often during
the day the need for prayer and
take trouble to pray. God is always
speaking to us. Listen to Him.
He wants from us deep love,
compassion and forgiveness.

$\mathcal{T}$he suffering in the refugee camps
is great. It all looks like one big
Calvary where Christ is crucified
once more. Help is needed
but unless there is forgiveness,
there will be no peace.

*O*n the old Yugoslavia' situation :
Our mission is not one of politics
but of love, and the truth is that
bitterness solves nothing.
Our message is one of peace and
reconciliation because the alternative
is a conflict which produces hunger,
suffering, anger and hate for all.

*I*f peace and love are not allowed
to take their rightful place at the
table of negotiation, then hatred
and anger will produce a conflict
that will continue for many
years to come. It will solve nothing
and thousands of innocent lives
will be lost. I ask you all to
pray for peace which is such
an urgent priority.

*W*here man has failed,
God will find a way —
if we ask Him.

*M*y Sisters and I always greet the
Lord and one another each morning
at 4.30 a.m. with the words :
'Let us bless the Lord
Thanks be to God.'
Let us always greet each other with
a smile — for a smile is the
beginning of love.

*T*he future is not in our hands.
We have no power over it.
We can act only today.
We have a sentence in
our Constitution that says :
'We will allow the good God to
make plans for the future — for
yesterday has gone, tomorrow
has not yet come and we have
only today to make Him
known, loved and served.'
So we do not worry about it.

*T*he greatest injustice we have done to our poor people is that we think they are good for nothing; we have forgotten to treat them with respect, with dignity as a child of God. People have forgotten what the human touch is, what it is to smile, for somebody to smile at them, somebody to recognize them, somebody to wish them well. The terrible thing is to be unwanted.

*I*t is easy to be proud and harsh
and selfish — so easy. But we have
been created for better things.
Each of us has plenty of good
as well as plenty of bad in us.
Let none glory in his or her success
but refer all to God.

*W*hy do people come to India?
Because they believe that in India
we have a lot of spirituality and this
they want to find. Among them are
many who come to our house
and work with us, in the
Home for the Dying.
Many of them are completely lost;
it is very important that they are
guided, that they are led.
Why are people going round in
circles, just to see the scenery?
There is not much point in that —
but there is something more;
people are really hungry for God.
Travel is one way of showing
their hunger.

A young girl came from a
university in Paris and she had told
her parents : 'Before I sit for my
final examination I want to go to
Mother Teresa and work with her.'
She came to Calcutta and I looked
at her. She looked very tired, her
eyes were not smiling. I suggested
that she come for the Adoration
that we have every day and that
she keep up regular visits to the
Home for the Dying. Then one day,
after ten or twelve visits,
she suddenly came and threw her
arms around me and said :
'Mother Teresa, I have found Jesus.'
I asked : Where did you find Jesus?
'In the Home for the Dying,'
she replied. She was full of
joy and smiles.

I think of you and your families
and pray for each one of you :
Lord, keep them faithful to each
other in Your love.
Let nothing, nobody separate
them from Your love and love
for each other.
Let the child, the gift of Yourself to
every family, be the bond of love,
unity, joy and peace.
Amen.

August

*G*od is joy, joy is prayer.
Joy is a sign of generosity.
When you are full of joy, you move
faster and you want to go about
doing good to everyone.
Joy is a sign of union with God —
of God's presence.

A little child has no difficulty in loving, has no obstacles to love. And that is why Jesus said : 'Unless you become like little children you cannot enter the kingdom of God.'

*T*he most natural thing is the
family life. What keeps the family
together, what nourishes the life of
the family together,
is that surrender to each other;
is that obedience;
is that accepting of each other.

*I*f there is not that obedience and
surrender of the father and mother
to each other, there can be very
little courage in the parents to ask
that obedience of their children.
And if today we are having all the
troubles with family life, I think it
begins there.

I was surprised to see so many
young boys and girls given to
drugs. And I tried to find out why.
And the answer was: Because in
the family there is no one to
receive them. Our children depend
on us for everything — their health,
their mission, their nutrition, their
security, their coming to know and
love God. For all of this they look
to us with trust, hope and
expectation. We are talking of love
of the child, which is where love
and peace begin.

*O*nce I picked up a child and took him to our Children's Home, gave him a bath, clean clothes, everything. After a day the child ran away. He was found by somebody else but again he ran away. Then I said to the Sisters : Please follow the child and see where he goes when he runs away. And the child ran away the third time.

There under a tree was the mother. She had put a small earthenware vessel on two stones and was cooking something she had picked out of the dustbin. The Sisters asked the child : 'Why did you run away from the Home?'

And the child said :

'This is my home because this is where my mother is.'

Mother was there. That was home.

*S*ilence is the beautiful fruit of
prayer. We must learn not only the
silence of the mouth
but also the silence of the heart,
of the eyes, of the ears and
of the mind, which I call the
five silences. Say it and memorize it
on your five fingers.

*D*o not imagine that love to be
true must be extraordinary. No,
what we need in our love is the
continuity to love the One we love.
See how a lamp burns, by the
continual consumption of little
drops of oil. If there are no more
of these drops in the lamp,
there will be no light.

*W*hat are these drops of oil in
our lamps? They are the little things
of everyday life : fidelity,
little words of kindness,
just a little thought for others,
those little acts of silence,
of look and thought,
of word and deed.

I always say I am a little pencil in
God's hands. He does the thinking.
He does the writing. He does
everything and sometimes it is really
hard because it is a broken pencil
and He has to sharpen it a little
more. Be a little instrument in His
hands so that He can use you any
time, anywhere. We have only to
say 'yes' to God.

*W*hen once a chairman of a
multinational company came to see
me, to offer me a property in
Bombay, he first asked :
'Mother, how do you manage your
budget?' I asked him who had sent
him here. He replied :
'I felt an urge inside me.'
I said : Other people like you come
to see me and say the same.
It was clear God sent you, Mr A, as
He sends Mr X, Mrs Y, Miss Z, and
they provide the material means we
need for our work. The grace of
God is what moved you. You are
my budget. God sees to our needs,
as Jesus promised. I accepted the
property he gave and named it
Asha Dan (Gift of Hope).

*T*his is the prayer by Newman that I once gave to the President of India and which he said gave him consolation in times of stress and difficulty : 'Dear Jesus, help me to spread your fragrance everywhere I go. Flood my soul with your spirit and life. Penetrate and possess my whole being so utterly that all my life may only be a radiance of yours. Shine through me, and be so in me that every soul I come in contact with may feel your presence in my soul. Let them look up and see no longer me, but only Jesus.'

*P*rayer by J.H Newman :
'Stay with me, and then I shall
begin to shine as you shine;
so to shine as to be a light to
others; the light O Jesus, will be
mine; it will be shining on others
through me. Let me thus praise you
in the way you love best,
by shining on those around me.
Let me preach to you without
preaching, not by words but by my
example, by the catching force, the
sympathetic influence of what I do;
the evident fullness of the love my
heart bears to you. Amen.'

*T*o be able to see the face of God you need a heart that is completely pure, clean and free. As long as we in our own hearts are not able to hear that voice, the voice of God when He speaks in the silence of our hearts, we will not be able to pray, we will not be able to express our love in action.

*T*o business people, Lions,
Rotarians, Knights and others who
come with generous cheques :
I hope that what you give me
comes not from your surplus but it
is the fruit of a sacrifice made for
the love of God. You must give
what costs you, go without
something you like, then you will
truly be brothers to the poor
who are deprived of even the
things they need.

Let us raise funds of love, of kindness, of understanding, of peace and again let us begin in the place where we are with the people with whom we are the closest, and then spread out. So let us protect this work, this mission, from anything that will make people think we are raising money except out of sacrifice.

*Y*ou are a rich nation but on your
streets I saw a man lying drunk
and no one picked him up,
no one seemed to bother about
him, no one tried to restore to him
his human dignity, to bring back to
him the sense that he is a brother,
a child of God.

For all kinds of diseases there are medicines and cures. But for the disease of being unwanted, except where there are willing hands to serve and there is a loving heart to love, I don't think this terrible disease can ever be cured.

*I*t is not how much we really 'have' to give but how empty we are — so that we can receive fully in our life. Take away your eyes from yourself and rejoice that you have nothing — that you are nothing — that you can do nothing. Give Jesus a big smile each time your nothingness frightens you.

$\mathcal{W}$e all speak of the terrible hunger that has been in Ethiopia, that has been in other places, where people in hundreds and thousands are facing death just for a piece of bread, for a glass of water. People have died in my hands. And yet we forget, why they and not we?

*I*f I had just passed by when I saw
and smelt that woman who was
eaten up by rats — her face, her
legs, I could not have been a
Missionary of Charity today. But I
returned, picked her up and took
her to a local hospital. If I had not,
the Society would have died.
Feelings of repugnance are human
but if I see the face of Jesus in His
distressing disguise, I will be holy.

*E*very child has been created for
greater things, to love and be loved,
in the image of God. That's why
people must decide from
beforehand if they really want to
have a child. Once a child is
conceived, there is life, God's life.
That child has a right to live and
be cared for. Abortion destroys two
lives, the life of the child and the
conscience of the mother.
It is a child of God, no?
Created for greater things,
just like you or me.

*T*he other day, a group of school children came from very far. All the first and second prize winners in the school had asked the headmistress to give money instead of prizes. So she put all the money in an envelope and gave it to them.

Then they all said :

'Take us to Mother Teresa, we want to give this money to her poor people.'

Now see, how wonderful it was that they did not use the money for themselves.

*T*o my Sisters : To sit back with a stick in hand and command is not our work. Our children come on empty stomachs — so do not waste their time. They must learn something. Make them happy. They have much to suffer already and we cannot treat them as we would children going to a regular school. How many of our children have their first meal at 3 p.m. so as to be able to cut out dinner because their parents cannot afford it? We thoughtlessly say hurtful things to little ones, ignorant as we are of the circumstances, and they stop coming. Even the little consolation they hope to find in school is denied them.

I find that when I'm writing,
writing and writing, I use up the
pens so quickly. When the ink
begins to look very faint, the Sister
puts a new pen in my hand,
but I always give it back to her,
because I won't take anything
without asking permission.
Use these words : 'May I have'.

*W*e cannot share unless our lives
are filled with the love of God;
unless our hearts are pure. Jesus
said : 'Blessed are the clean of
heart for they shall see God.'
If we do not see God in each
other, it is very difficult to love.
And as love begins at home,
we must have that love for each
other at home.

A little boy in Calcutta was
celebrating his birthday. His parents
always gave him lots of presents
and a big party. One year he asked
them to give all the money they
would spend on him to
Mother Teresa. So on the morning
of the birthday, they brought him
down in a car and handed me an
envelope with the money in it.
The child taught his parents so
much. That is love in action.

*O*ne of the most demanding
things for me is travelling with all
the publicity everywhere I go.
I have said to Jesus if I don't go to
heaven for anything else,
I will be going to heaven for all the
travelling and the publicity,
because it has purified me and
sacrificed me and made me truly
ready for heaven.

*D*eath is going home, yet people
are afraid of what will come, so
they do not want to die. There is
also the question of conscience :
'I could have done better.'
Very often, as we live so we die.
Death is nothing but a continuation
of life, the completion of life, the
surrendering of the human body.
But the heart and the soul live
forever. They do not die.

*T*o parents : It is very important
that children learn from their fathers
and mothers how to love one
another — not in the school, not
from the teacher, but from you. It is
very important that you share with
your children the joy of that smile.
There will be misunderstandings;
every family has its cross, its
suffering. Always be the first to
forgive with a smile.

Be cheerful, be happy.

*P*eople all over the world are
hungry for God's love. Your way
of doing it is by spreading peace
and love and our way is by
putting that love into action in
the service of the sick, the dying
and the unwanted. Let us pray
for each other and help each other
by honesty and we shall conquer
the world and bring to the world
the message that God is love
and God loves each one of us
as we love one another.

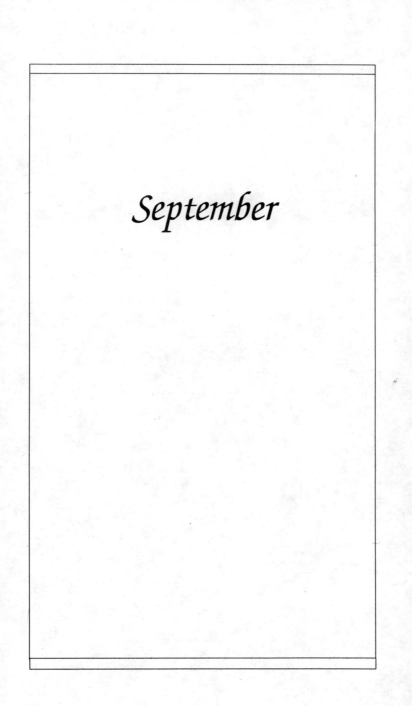

September

The other day I received $15 from a man who has been on his back for twenty years and the only part that he can move is his right hand. And the only companion that he enjoys is smoking.

And he said to me : 'I do not smoke for one week, and I send you this money.'

It must have been a terrible sacrifice for him but see how beautiful, how he shared. And with that money I brought bread and I gave to those who are hungry with a joy on both sides. He was giving and the poor were receiving.

*B*e kind and merciful. Let no one ever come to you without leaving better and happier. Be a living expression of God's kindness : kindness in your face, kindness in your eyes, kindness in your smile, kindness in your warm greeting. To children, to the poor, to all who suffer and are lonely, give always a happy smile. Give them not only your care, but also your heart.

*T*he presence of the nuclear bomb
in the world has created fear and
distrust among nations as it is one
more weapon to destroy human life,
which is God's beautiful presence in
the world. How can peace be
established? Only if we love each
other. The greedy who are fighting
for power and money do not know
love and love alone can help
establish peace in the family,
in society and in the world.

*T*o students : The wise observation by Pope Pius XII that the direction that society will take tomorrow depends mainly on the minds and hearts of today's university students, is an invitation to you to be aware of the privilege and the responsibility that so many of you have today, as young people in an institute of learning. The university offers you a whole array of excellent means for completing your formation. You must not, however, think of yourself alone. You are called to build up human society. As university students you have at your disposal abundant means that you must learn to know and appreciate fully.

*W*e must be able to make a
distinction between self-knowledge
and sin. Self-knowledge will help
one to rise up, whereas sin is a
weakness that leads to repeated sin
and despondency. Deep confidence
and trust will come through
self-knowledge. Then you will turn
to Jesus to support you in
your weakness whereas if you
think you are strong,
you will not need our Lord.

A rich man came to me and said he wanted to give up something in his life — his house, his car.
I suggested : When you go to the store to buy a new suit or some clothes, instead of buying the best, buy one that is a little less expensive and use that extra money to buy something for someone else, or better still for the poor. When I finished saying this he looked really amazed and exclaimed : 'Oh! Is that the way, Mother? I never thought of it.' When he left, he looked so happy and full of joy at the thought of helping others.

*W*here is God?
We believe He is everywhere —
He is the creator, He is everything.
But where is He
to my human eyes?
To make it possible for me to
see the face of God with my
human eyes, He has made Himself
the hungry one, the naked one,
the homeless one, the lonely one
and He says :
'Whatsoever you do to the least of
my brethren you do it to me.'
Gandhiji has said :
'He who serves the poor
serves God.'

*T*o my co-workers :
Keep giving Jesus to your people,
not by words but by your example,
by being in love with Jesus,
by radiating His holiness and
spreading His fragrance of love
everywhere you go.
Just keep the joy of Jesus as your
strength. Be happy and at peace.
You belong to him. Tell him :
'I am yours — and if you cut me to
pieces, every single piece will be
only yours.'

What made me start my work,
what inspired me and kept me
going during so many years?
Jesus. We do it for Jesus.
I take Jesus at His word and
He never lets me down.
He said : 'Ask and you will receive.'
So I ask. If it is for His glory He
will grant it, if not, let us forget
about it. God knows what is
good for us.

I was travelling by train to Darjeeling when I heard the voice of God. I was sure it was God's voice. I was certain He was calling me. The message was clear. I must leave the convent to help the poor by living among them. This was a command, something to be done, something definite. The call was something between God and me. What matters is that God calls each of us in a different way. In those difficult, dramatic days I was certain that this was God's doing and not mine and I am still certain. And it was the work of God. I knew that the world would benefit from it.

*O*ur expanding knowledge does not dim our faith, it only shows the size of God's creation. Often we cannot understand. There is a beautiful example in the life of St. Augustine who was struggling to understand God, to understand the Trinity, to understand the magnitude of God's creation. His human mind could not grasp it. Then he came upon a small boy who was trying to fill water in a hole in the ground. St. Augustine asked him what he was doing and the boy said : 'I am trying to fill this hole with water.' St. Augustine said that it was impossible. Then the child who, in truth, was an angel, said : 'It is still easier to put the ocean into this hole than for you to understand the mystery of God.'

*O*ne day while I was working, a
Sister came in and said : 'A tourist
wants to see you; he is the person
who came the other day.'
I said : Tell him to go and
work in Kalighat.
The Sister replied that he said he
had gone there yesterday.
Yes, I said, he can go again today;
the poor are still there.

*M*any people are deeply
concerned with the children of
India, with the children of Africa
where quite a few die of hunger.
Many people are also concerned
about all the violence in this great
country of the United States.
These concerns are very good.
But often these same people are
not concerned with the millions
who are being killed by the
deliberate decision of their own
mothers. And this is what is the
greatest destroyer of peace today —
abortion, which brings people to
such blindness.

*T*he care of the poor and needy is
not the responsibility of the State
only. It is the responsibility of
everyone. Every person must be
concerned with his brothers' and
sisters' needs.

*T*o know the problem of poverty
intellectually is not to understand it.
It is not by reading, taking a walk
in the slums, admiring and
regretting that we come to
understand it and to discover what
it has of bad and good. We have to
dive into it, live it, share it.

*T*o my helpers and volunteers :
Discover the other through direct
contact. Go to Kalighat, the Home
for the Dying, and learn your
lessons, not out of a book,
but in the rough and tumble of life,
among real people, in a setting
you will never forget.

*O*ne night in London I went out
visiting people with the Sisters. We
saw a young boy with long hair,
sitting in the street with others.
I spoke to him and I said : You
shouldn't be here, you should be
with your mother and father, this is
not the place for you. The young
boy said : 'My mother does not
want me. Each time I go home, she
pushes me out, because she can't
bear my long hair.' We passed on.
When I came back, he was lying
flat on the ground. He had
overdosed himself. We had to take
him to hospital. I could not help
but reflect : Here was a child
hungry for home, and his mother
had no time for him. This is great
poverty. This is where you and I
must make this world
a better world.

*I*f you have not the experience,
ask. There is no shame in asking,
but do not pretend you know
when you don't.

*T*he tide of human suffering grows ever greater. This is especially so of those who are refugees. Theirs is a special kind of suffering. Not only are they forced to suffer famine, persecution, war and natural disaster, but also the horrific plight of being forced to keep on the move. They have nowhere which they can call home and often no one is prepared to listen to their cry for help.

*T*o Him, each one of us is very
special, each one a unique creation.
We are one world.
We are all sisters and brothers in
Jesus Christ. We must work for
all those who suffer and hear
Our Lord say : 'I was a refugee and
you gave me a home.'

*E*very religion believes in
eternity — another life. This life on
earth is not the end. People who
believe it is the end, fear death.
If it was properly explained that
death was nothing but going
home to God, then there would be
no fear of death.

*T*he Minister of the Imperial Court
in Addis Ababa asked me a few
searching questions :
'What do you want from the
Government?'
Nothing. I have come only to offer
my Sisters to work among the poor
suffering people.
'What will your Sisters do?'
We give wholehearted free service
to the poorest of the poor.
'What qualifications do they have?'
We try to bring tender love and
compassion to the unwanted,
to the unloved.
'Do you preach to the people
trying to convert them?'
Our works of love reveal to the
suffering poor the love of God
for them.

*T*he greatest poverty in the world
is not the want of food but the
want of love. You have the poverty
of people who are dissatisfied with
what they have, who do not know
how to suffer, who give in to
despair. The poverty of the heart is
often more difficult to relieve and
to defeat.

*G*od has created us to love and to be loved, and this is the beginning of prayer — to know that he loves me, that I have been created for greater things.

*L*ove to be true has to begin
with God in prayer.
If we pray we will be able to love
and if we love, we will be able to
serve and therefore let us all
promise that we will give our hearts
to love them for they
too have been created for
greater things.

*C*ardinal Cooke made me an offer
of five hundred dollars a month
for each Sister working in Harlem
and I said to him :
Do you think that God is going to
be bankrupt in New York?
He provides the means.
So why do we worry?

*C*hildren long for somebody
to accept them,
to love them,
to praise them,
to be proud of them.
Let us bring the child back to the
centre of our care and concern.
This is the only way the world can
survive because our children are
the only hope for the future.
As older people are called to God,
only their children can take
their place.

*P*ray for the family with me : Heavenly Father, you have given us a model of life in the Holy Family of Nazareth. Help us, O Loving Father, to make our family another Nazareth where love, peace and joy reign, may it be deeply contemplative, intensely Eucharistic and vibrant with joy. Help us to stay together in joy and sorrow through family prayer. Teach us to see Jesus in the members of our family especially in their distressing disguise.

The fruit of prayer is a clean heart
and a clean heart is free to love.
The fruit of love is
Peace — Unity — Joy.

*W*e do more harm than good to young healthy people when we give them things. It encourages them to beg. Always see that they do not depend on what you give them. We must teach them something — needlework, typing, dressmaking. We must also teach them the love of the home — to make beautiful the little they have.

October

*L*ove is a fruit, in season at all times and within the reach of every hand. Anyone may gather it and no limit is set. Everyone can reach this love through meditation, the spirit of prayer and sacrifice.

God doesn't ask that we succeed
in everything, but that we are
faithful. However beautiful our work
may be, let us not become attached
to it. Always remain prepared to
give it up, without losing
your peace.

*T*oday we see more and more
that all the suffering in the world
has started from the home.
Today we have no time even to
look at each other, to talk to each
other, to enjoy each other, and still
less to be what our children expect
from us, what the husband expects
from the wife, what the wife
expects from the husband.
And so more and more we are out
of our homes and less and less
in touch with each other.

*R*iches and money do not make us rich — what makes us rich is our attachment to them. God gives us things to share, God doesn't give us things to hold, and so the more we learn to share the more we come to know each other, we will love one another, and if we love one another we will be able to share the joy of what we have.

I will never forget the night an old
gentleman came to our house and
said that there was a family with
eight children and they had not
eaten, and would we do something
for them. So I took some rice and
went there. The mother took the
rice from my hands, then she
divided it into two and went out.
I could see the faces of the
children shining with hunger.
When she came back I asked her
where she had gone.
She gave me a very simple answer :
'They are hungry also.'
And 'they' were the family next
door and she knew that they were
hungry. I was not surprised that she
gave, but I was surprised that she
knew.

*A*nd this is something that is so
beautiful to see, that shining
happiness in the face of that
mother, who had the love to share.
I had not the courage to ask her
how long her family hadn't eaten,
but I am sure it must have been a
long time, and yet she knew —
in her suffering, in her sorrow,
in her terrible bodily suffering
she knew that next door they
were hungry also.
Do we know that our neighbour
needs love? Do we know that our
neighbour needs care?
As the example of this family
shows, God will never forget us
and there is something you and I
can always do.

*J*oy is prayer, joy is strength, joy is
love. God loves a cheerful giver.
The best way we can show our
gratitude to God and the people is
to accept everything with joy.

*H*ow much love do we put
in our presents? That's why people
who have not got the capacity
to give and to receive love,
even if they are very rich,
are the poorest of the poor.

*W*henever you feel that you have
not done something, do not be
afraid. He is a loving Father. God's
mercy is much greater than we can
imagine. The Sisters also need your
prayers to be able to do their work;
the poor need your help,
your understanding, your love.
We all have much to give,
to share, to contribute,
wherever we find ourselves.

*H*oliness is not the luxury reserved for a few favourite persons. All are invited to be holy. I think only holiness will be able to overcome evil and all the sufferings and miseries of the people, and of our own lives. Because we too have to suffer, and suffering is a gift of God if we use it in the right way.

The cross must be there, so let us thank God for this.

*W*e are not channels, we are
instruments. Channels give nothing
of their own, they just let water run
through them. In our action, we are
instruments in God's hand and
He writes beautifully.

*T*o doctors : Yours is a consecrated
life, because touching the sick,
in healing the sick, Jesus said :
'You did it to me.' How full of love
your heart must be, because the
sick, the lonely, the disabled come
to you with hope and that is why
they must be able to receive
from you that tender love,
that compassion.

*S*omeone asked me :
What will you do when you are
not Mother General any more?'
I replied : I am first-class at
cleaning toilets and drains.
It is not what we do,
but how much love we put
into the doing. If I belong to
Christ and at that moment He wants
me to be cleaning the toilets, or
taking care of the sufferers from
leprosy, or talking to the
President of the United States, it is
all the same; because I am being
what God wants me to be, and
doing what He wants me to do.
I belong to Him.

*Y*oung people, open your hearts to
the love of God. He loves you with
tenderness, and He will give you
not just to give but to share. And
the less you have, the more you
can give; and the more you have,
the less you can give.
And so, when you are praying ask,
ask for courage,
and give and give until it hurts.
This kind of giving is love
in action.

I find the work much easier and I
can smile more sincerely when
I think of each one of my suffering
brothers and sisters.
Jesus needs you to keep pouring
into the lamp of your life the oil
of your love and sacrifice.
You are really reliving the passion
of Christ. Bruised, divided, full of
pain and wounds as you are, accept
Jesus as He comes into your life.

Yesterday is gone. Tomorrow is yet
to come. We have only today.
If we help our children to be what
they should be today, they will
have the necessary courage to face
life with greater love.

*S*ilence is the root of our union
with God and with one another.
In silence we are filled with the
energy of God Himself that makes
us do all things in joy. The more
we receive in silent prayer, the
more we can give in our active life.

*I*t is better to make mistakes in kindness than to work miracles with unkindness. It is very important to be kind to ourselves and control ourselves by keeping our balance. If we want to live in peace and harmony with each other we must pay attention to our tongue. Especially when we deal with the poor we must be very careful in talking to them.

*I*t strikes me how God is humble.
He humbled Himself; He who
possessed the fullness of the
Godhead took the form of a
servant. Even today God shows
His humility by making use of
instruments as weak and imperfect
as we are. He deigns to work
through us. Then there must be joy
in the heart. That is not
incompatible with humility.

*T*o doctors : You cannot love the patients and the suffering if you have no love for your own at home. That is why, not only must you try to love, you *must* love. That is why, before you touch a patient, before you listen to the patient — pray. Because you need a clean heart to love that patient. And you need clean hands to touch that patient. I will pray for you that, through this work of your hands and heart you may grow in holiness. Let us promise our Lord that through your medical work, you are going to become holy.

*T*o Rotarians, Lions and Knights :
You are men with influence; you
have power; you have money;
use them well for the good of
society, especially for the
benefit of the poor.

I find it great, great poverty that a
child must die because we are
afraid to feed one more child,
to educate one more child.
The fear of feeding one more old
person in the family means that that
person must be put away, and yet
one day we too have to meet the
Master. What will we answer to him
about that little child, that old father
and mother, because they are His
creation, they are children of God.

*T*his is what is so beautiful for
you, young people. Open your
hearts to the love of God which
He will give you. He loves you
with tenderness. And He will give
you not to keep but to share.
And the less you have, the more
you can give and the more you
have, the less you can give.
And so when we are praying,
ask — ask for courage to
give until it hurts.

*T*o young people who say :
'I could never do that — I'm no
Mother Teresa,' I would tell them
that they need a clean heart and
we get a clean heart by praying.
That's the beginning of great love.
They will be able with a clean
heart to see Jesus in the poor and
do everything that Christ wants
them to do : feed the hungry,
clothe the naked, house the
homeless. Because it is only for
love. And the young people today
don't want to listen so much as
they want to see, to see love in
action, to see faith in action.

*D*eep confidence and trust will come through self-knowledge. Then you will turn to Jesus to support your weakness, whereas if you think you are strong, you will not need our Lord. Do your very best to reduce self-will. Don't do anything just for yourself; concentrate on the whole, in which you are included. Then you will be able to receive God's grace.

When I choose evil, I sin.
That's where my will comes in.
When I seek something for myself
at the cost of everything else,
I deliberately choose sin.
For example, I am tempted to tell a
lie and then I accept to tell the
lie. I have put an obstacle between
me and God. That lie has won.
I preferred to lie to God.

*T*o love and be loved, we must
know our brothers and our sisters,
for knowledge always leads to love,
and love in action is service.
Our work is only the expression of
the love we have for God.

*E*ach one of us is here today because we have been loved by God who created us and our parents who accepted and cared enough to give us life. Life is the most beautiful gift of God. That is why it is so painful to see what is happening today in so many places around the world; life being deliberately destroyed by war, by violence, by abortion.

*W*e picked up a young man from the streets of Calcutta. He was very highly educated and had many degrees. He had fallen into bad hands and his passport had been stolen. After sometime, I asked him why he had left home. He said his father did not want him. 'From childhood he never looked me in the eye. He became jealous of me, so I left home.' After much praying, the Sisters helped him to return home to forgive his father and this helped both of them. This is a case of very great poverty.

*L*et me tell you something :
If you feel the weight of your sins,
do not be afraid!
He is a loving Father;
God's mercy is much greater than
we can imagine.

*H*umility is the mother of all
virtues; purity, charity and
obedience. It is in being humble
that our love becomes real, devoted
and ardent. If you are humble
nothing will touch you,
neither praise nor disgrace,
because you know what you are.
If you are blamed you will not
be discouraged. If they call you
a saint you will not put yourself
on a pedestal.

November

*I*n God we live and move and
have our being.
It is God who gives life to all,
who gives power and being to all
that exists. But for His sustaining
presence, all things would cease to
be and fall back into nothingness.
Consider that you are in God,
surrounded and encompassed
by God, swimming in God.

*W*hen a foundation was started
in Venezuela, some of the young
Sisters felt thrilled but nervous and
asked : 'How shall we manage
in a new country of which we
know neither the language
nor the customs?'
I told them :
Fear not, little ones, you speak a
language all men understand,
the language of charity.
To the question :
'What are you taking?' I replied :
Our hearts and our hands.

*L*ove can be misused for selfish motives. I love you but at the same time I want to take from you as much as I can, even the things that are not for me to take. Then there is no true love any more.

*J*esus has said that we are much
more important to His Father than
the grass, the birds, the flowers of
the earth; and so if He takes such
care of these things,
how much more would He take
care of His life in us.
He cannot deceive us;
because life is God's greatest gift
to human beings; for since the
unborn child is created in the image
of God it belongs to Him; and we
have no right to destroy it.

*B*y abortion, the mother kills even her own child to solve her problems. And, by abortion, the father is told that he does not have to take any responsibility at all for the child he has brought into the world. That father is likely to put other women into the same trouble. So abortion leads to abortion. Any country that accepts abortion is not teaching its people to love but to use violence to get what they want. This is why the greatest destroyer of love and peace is abortion.

*H*ow do we love? Not in big things but in small things with great love. There is so much love in us all. We must not be afraid to show our love.

*Y*ou, today, as young people —
some are studying, some are
working, some are preparing for the
future — have that conviction, have
that tender love for Christ, and with
Him and through Him you will be
able to do great things.
But to be able to do that,
we need to pray, and the fruit of
prayer is deepening of faith,
and the fruit of faith is love,
and the fruit of love is service.

We are able to go through the
most terrible places fearlessly,
because Jesus in us will never
deceive us; Jesus in us is our love,
our strength, our joy and our
compassion.

*I*n Beirut when I wanted to go
across the lines and fetch the
children, I was reminded that I
would have to cross the fighting
lines and may be shot at.
I insisted : No, tomorrow there will
be a truce — the fighting will stop.
The Sisters have prayed that there
will be a ceasefire and truce
tomorrow. And so it was. We took
charge of the orphaned and
crippled children and brought them
safely home.

L et us all pray especially that
people shall be brothers and sisters
in the world and will understand
this prayer. We can each think
about it separately and examine our
conscience. And each of us before
we pass the prayer on to somebody
else, let us put this prayer into life :
Lead me from death to life,
from falsehood to truth;
Lead me from despair to hope,
from fear to trust;
Lead me from hate to love,
from war to peace;
Let peace fill our heart,
our world, our universe.

*O*ur purpose is to take God and
His love to the poorest of the poor,
irrespective of their ethnic origin
or the faith they profess.
Our discernment of aid is not the
belief but the necessity. In our
work we bear witness to the love
of God's presence and if Catholics,
Protestants, Buddhists or agnostics
become for this reason better
men — simply better — we will be
satisfied. Growing up in God's love
they will be nearer to God and will
find Him in His goodness.

*T*o my co-workers :
I would like you to concentrate
more in giving wholehearted free
service to the poor in your own
area. Each one of you try to find
out the lonely, the unwanted, the
handicapped. Maybe just a smile,
a small visit, just to light the fire
for someone, read for somebody.
Small, yes, very small. But that will
be your love of God in action. This
spirit must radiate from your own
heart to your family, neighbour,
town, country, the world.

A mission of love can come
only from union with God.
From that union, love for the
family, love for neighbour,
love for the poor is natural fruit.

A Brazilian gentleman who held a high position, wrote to me that he had lost total faith in God and in man, and he had given up everything, and only wanted to commit suicide. One day, passing by a shop, his eyes had suddenly fallen on the TV and there was a scene from the Home for the Dying in Kalighat — the Sisters looking after the sick and the dying. He wrote to me after seeing that scene that for the first time after many years he knelt down and prayed. Now he has decided to turn back to God and have faith in humanity because he saw that God still loves the world and he saw this on TV.

My TV is the tabernacle.

*T*o my Sisters : Our children may be only slum children but for that very reason just anything will not do. Each Sister must find a way to attract and capture the children. Do not think that you need not prepare yourself because you know more than they. They must have the best, and their good must be uppermost in your mind. Do not stale in your method, like stagnant water . . . . Keep on improving but you must also know how to impart it. Never put off preparation as something trivial. The happiness of the children should be our main concern — and at the same time learn the most necessary things.

*B*e sincere in your prayer.
Do you know how to pray?
Do you pray your prayers?
Do you love to pray?
When we come face to face with
God we cannot but be sincere and
know ourselves — that we are
nothing. It is only when we realize
our nothingness, our emptiness, that
God can fill us with himself. When
we become full of God we will do
all our work well.

*N*obody in the Home for the
Dying in Kalighat has died
depressed, in despair, unwanted,
unfed or unloved. That is why I
think this is the treasure house of
Calcutta. We try and give them
whatever they want — according to
what is written in the book, be it
Hindu, or Muslim, or Buddhist or
Catholic or Protestant, or any other
Society. The religious societies
collect their own dead and provide
them cremation or burial according
to their religious rites. Some ask for
Ganges water, some for holy water,
for a word or a prayer.
Some just ask for an apple
or a pomegranate or a cigarette.
Others want somebody
to sit by them.

*W*hen you believe you love,
when you love, you want to give
your service, to give yourself.
God gave us an example :
He gives us everything freely;
we must also give what we have,
give ourselves.
Let there be no pride or vanity
in the work.
Whatever we give them, make sure
we have it to give.

*A*m I ever angry or frustrated?
I only feel angry sometimes when
I see waste, when things
that we waste are what people
need, things that would save
them from dying.
Frustrated? No, never.

*W*hy these people and not me?
That person picked up from the
drain, why is he here, why not me?
That is the mystery.
Nobody can give that answer.
Where there is a mystery,
there must be faith. Faith you
cannot change no matter how you
look at it. Either you have it
or you don't.

*F*aith is a gift of God.
Without it there would be no life.
And our work, to be fruitful and
beautiful, has to be built on faith.
Love and faith go together.
They complete each other.

I was asked why I did not give a
rod with which to fish, in the hands
of the poor, rather than give the
fish itself as this makes them
remain poor. So I told them :
The people whom we pick up are
not able to stand with a rod.
So today I will give them fish and
when they are able to stand,
then I shall send them to you and
you can give them the rod.
That is your job.
Let me do my work today.

*I*f we have difficulties in our family
life, if we have so much struggle in
our family life, it is because life in
the family is broken, and it is
broken by our own hands.
And the destruction is coming
from within. If it came from
outside, it would be easy to push it
out; but when it's coming from
inside, then it is very difficult.
And that's why I think
we need to pray.

*T*here should be less talk;
a preaching point is not always
a meeting point. What do you
do then? Take a broom and clean
someone's house. That says enough.
All of us are but His instruments
who do our little bit and pass by.

*W*hether one is a Hindu or a
Muslim or a Christian, how you live
your life is proof that you are or
not fully His.
We cannot condemn or judge or
pass words that will hurt people.
We don't know in what way God is
appearing to that soul and what
God is drawing that soul to;
therefore, who are we to
condemn anybody?

*C*harity for the poor is like a
living flame; the drier the fuel, the
brighter it burns. In your service to
the poor do not give only your
hands but also your hearts.
Charity to be fruitful
must cost us.

*I*n Melbourne, I visited an old man
nobody seemed to know existed.
I saw his room; it was in a terrible
state. I wanted to clean it, but he
kept on saying : 'I'm all right.'
I didn't say a word, yet in the end
he allowed me to clean his room.
There was in that room a beautiful
lamp, covered for many years
with dust. I asked him :
Why do you not light the lamp?
'For whom?' he said. 'No one comes
to me.' I said : Will you light the
lamp if a Sister comes to see you?
He said : 'Yes, if I hear a human
voice, I will do it.' The other day,
he sent me word : 'Tell my friend
that the light she has lighted in
my life is still burning.'
See what a little act can do?

*D*earest Lord, may I see You today and every day in the person of Your sick, and, whilst nursing them, minister unto You. Though You hide yourself behind the unattractive disguise of the irritable, the exacting, the unreasonable, may I still recognize You, and say : 'Jesus, my patient, how sweet it is to serve You.'

I was in Beirut and was taken to a
bombed hospital where we found
fifty-five children of whom some
were severely handicapped. I said
that I would take the children.
We left for the convent with them,
though we were lacking everything,
even the necessities to care for
them. Some children and young
people (Muslims, Christians, Druses
etc.) came to help us and the
smallest went home to bring their
clothes to give these children.
Some were chewing gum and in
a burst of love, took the gum
that they were chewing and gave
it to them!

*I*f anyone wants to help me,
let them begin at home. There is
help needed on your doorstep,
in your place of work, in your
office and in your factory.
Once I went with the head of a big
company to his factory in Bombay
where over 3,000 people were
working. He had started a scheme
among them, where they all gave
something to feed the people in
Asha Dan, our home. I had gone
there to thank them and to my
surprise I found that many of his
employees were disabled. I was
also struck that he knew nearly all
of the workers by name and as we
went through the factory, he had
some greeting or word to say to
everyone. Thoughtfulness comes
when there is true love. Never be
so busy as not to think of others.

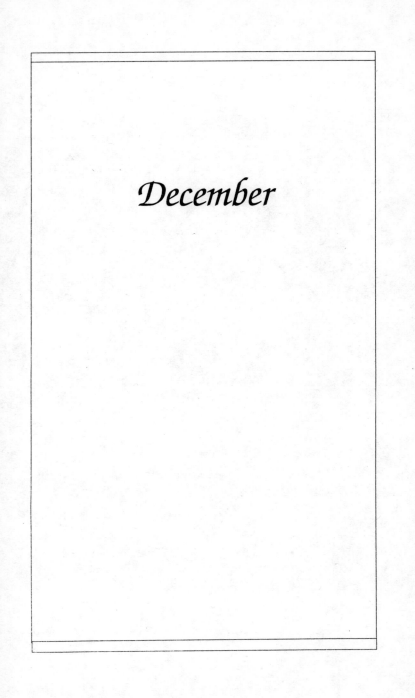

December

*L*et us pray for peace, joy and
love. We are reminded that Jesus
came to bring the good news :
'My peace I leave with you,
my peace I give to you.'
He came not to give the peace of
the world which is only that
we do not harm each other.
He came to give the peace of heart
which comes from loving —
from doing good to others.

We do not need guns and bombs to bring peace, we need love and compassion. Let us radiate the peace of God and so light His light and extinguish all hatred and love of power in the world and in the hearts of all men.

At the Home for the Dying in
Kalighat, a visitor wondered at the
peace that pervaded everywhere.
I told him : God is here.
Castes and creeds mean nothing.
It does not matter that they
are not of my faith.

*I*f you are discouraged it is
a sign of pride because it shows
you trust in your own power.
Your self-sufficiency, your
selfishness and your intellectual
pride will inhibit His coming to live
in your heart because God cannot
fill what is already full. It is
as simple as that.

*W*e need to find God and He
cannot be found in noise and
restlessness. God is a friend of
silence. The more we engage
in silent prayer, the more we
can give in our active life.
The essential thing is not what
we say but what God says to us
and what He says through us.

Sometime ago, two young people came to our house and they gave me a large sum of money to feed the poor. I asked them : Where did you get so much money?' And they said : 'Two days ago we got married and we decided that we were not going to buy wedding clothes, we were not going to have a wedding feast, we would give you the money to feed the poor.' And I asked them again : But why did you do that? They said : 'We love each other so much that we wanted to begin our life together by sharing the joy of loving with the people you serve by making a sacrifice.' This love is sanctity and the more we grow in this love, the closer we come to God.

*M*aybe in our own family we
have somebody who is feeling
lonely, who is feeling sick, who
is feeling worried. Are we there?
Let us know the poor in our own
families first. We have old people :
they are put in institutions and they
are never visited; with less and less
time even to smile at each other,
with less and less time to be
together. Love begins at home,
if we can only make our
own homes temples of love.

I hope I am converting people. I don't mean what you think. I hope we are converting hearts. Not even Almighty God can convert a person unless that person wants it. What we are all trying to do by our work, by serving the people, is to come closer to God. And this is the way conversion has to be understood — people think that conversion is changing overnight. It is not like that. If in coming face to face with God we accept Him in our lives, then we are converting. We become better Hindus, better Muslims, better Catholics, better whatever we are, and then by being better we come closer to Him.

*W*hat approach would I use?
It would naturally be a Catholic
one. For you it may be Hindu, for
someone else, Buddhist, according
to one's conscience. What God is in
your mind you must accept. But I
cannot prevent myself from giving
you what I have.

Some people came to Calcutta,
and before leaving, they begged
me : Tell us something that will
help us to live our lives better. And
I said : Smile at each other; smile at
your wife, smile at your husband,
smile at your children, smile at each
other — it doesn't matter who it is
and that will help you to grow in
greater love for each other.
And one of them asked me :
'Are you married?' I said : Yes, and
sometimes I find it very difficult
to smile at my spouse, Jesus,
because he can be very demanding.
This is really something true.
And that is where love comes in —
when it is demanding,
and yet we can give it with joy.

*D*o I need to pray?
Do I want to pray?
Remember wherever you may be —
Mother Teresa's prayer, love and
blessing will always be with you.
God bless you.

*I*f you have a sick or lonely
person at home, be there. Maybe
just to hold a hand, maybe just to
give a smile, that is the greatest,
the most beautiful work.

The poor people whom we gather each day are those whom society rejects and abandons. People do not think that the poor can be treated as people like you or I. We try to give human dignity back to them.

One day a young boy, 15 or 16 years old, came crying and begged me to give him some soap. I knew the family of that boy was rich and had become poor. He said to me : 'My sister goes to high school and every day she is sent back because her sari is not washed and we do not have soap to wash it. Please give me some soap so that she can wash her sari and she can go to school and finish her education.' Now we see the humiliation the family had to suffer because they were poor.

A smile must always be on our
lips for any child to whom we
offer help, for any to whom we
give companionship or medicine.
It would be very wrong to offer
only our cures; we must offer
to all our hearts.

'Lord, make me an instrument of your peace' is our motto. The most important part is that we keep the work as His work and that we do not spoil it by any claims. It is impossible, humanly speaking, for our young and inexperienced Sisters to do what they do but for the fact that we are just instruments to do God's work. Our task is to allow Jesus to use us. It is He who is doing the work with us, through us and in us.

*A*m I convinced of God's love
for me and mine for Him?
This conviction is like a sunlight
which makes the sap of life rise
and the buds of sanctity bloom.
This conviction is the rock on
which sanctity is built.

A Hindu woman married to a Parsi, came to ask for my blessings for her three-year-old son who could not speak. I asked the woman : Is there anything to which you are very attached, something dear to you? The child's mother replied : 'Yes, chewing betel. With me it has become a compulsory habit.' Give it up. Offer it to God as a sacrifice and pray for your son's cure, I said. She did and three months later her son started to speak and slowly became normal.

*B*e faithful in little things, for in them our strength lies. We may not be able to give much but we can always give the joy that springs in a heart that is in love with God.

I did not know that our work
would grow so fast or go so far. I
never doubted that it would live but
I did not think it would be like
this. Doubt I never had because
I had this conviction that if God
blesses it, it will prosper. Because
none of us have got the experience.
None of us have got the things the
world looks for. This is the miracle
of all these little Sisters all around
the world. God is using them;
as long as any of us have this
conviction, we are all right.
The work will prosper.

*I*n the Scriptures it is written :
'What will it profit, if a man says
he has faith, but does not have
works?' Can faith alone save him? If
a brother or a sister is naked and
in want of daily food and one of
you says to them: 'Go in peace, be
warmed and filled,' yet you do not
give them what is necessary for the
body, what does it profit?
So faith unless it has works is
dead in itself.

*I*f you really belong to the work
that has been entrusted to you, then
you must do it with your whole
heart. It is not how much we are
doing but how much honesty, how
much faith is put into doing it.
It makes no difference what we are
doing. Only sometimes we forget
and we spend more time looking at
somebody else and wishing we
were doing something else.

*G*od has blessed our society with
many vocations. We have many,
many young people who have
consecrated their lives to serve
Christ in the poorest of the poor —
to give their all to him — and it
has been a wonderful gift of God
to the whole world that through
this work, the rich and the poor
have come to know each other,
to love each other and to share
the joy of living by putting their
love, their understanding love,
into living action.

*O*ur vocation is to belong to
Jesus, not to work for the poor.
The work for the poor is our love
for God in action.
It is your vocation to have a family,
to love one another and the service
you do is your
love for God in action.

*T*he poor people are great people.
They can teach us so many
beautiful things. The other day one
of the poor people came to thank
us and said : 'You people who
have evolved chastity, you are the
best people to teach us family
planning because it is nothing
more than self-control out of love
for each other.'

*A*t Christmas, we see Jesus as a little babe — helpless and poor. And He came to love and be loved. How can we love Jesus in the world today? By loving Him in my husband, my wife, my children, my brothers and sisters, my parents, my neighbours and the poor. Let us gather around the poor crib in Bethlehem and make a strong resolution that we will love Jesus in all those we meet every day.

*T*he children in our homes in
Calcutta were given an early
Christmas treat one year by an
international airline which gave
them a free one-hour ride. I wish
you could have seen the excitement
of these 150 children, looking so
neat in matching shirts and caps
that had been donated for the
occasion. How wonderful that our
handicapped and malnourished
and abandoned children, who
would otherwise never have
experienced the joy of flying,
were given the chance.

I repeat that the poor, the sufferers
from leprosy, the rejected, the
alcoholics, whom we serve, are
beautiful people. Many of them
have wonderful personalities.
The experience which we have by
serving them, we must pass on to
people who have not had that
wonderful experience.

*T*he most important rule of a well-regulated family, of a family founded on love and unity, is that the children show an unbounded trust in and obedience to their parents. Jesus practiced this for thirty years in Nazareth for we hear nothing of Him but that 'he was subject to them,' that is, He did what He was told.

*T*oday, more than ever, we need
to pray for the light to know the
will of God . . . . for the love to
accept the will of God . . . .
for the way to do the will of God.

*A*t the Silver Jubilee of the
Congregation in Calcutta people
prayed for us and with us. We
went to pray with Hindus, Jains,
Sikhs, Buddhists, Zoroastrians, Jews,
Anglicans, Protestants, in fact with
people of all denominations and
religions in eighteen different
places. We concentrated on practical
devotion. We would get the top
people in firms and important
members of society to see the poor,
befriend them, come in contact with
them, learn their condition;
then they would serve them with
their own hands.
The poor were astonished and
deeply· moved when seeing such
well-dressed people come down
to serve them. Such an example
goes a long way.

*I*nstead of death and sorrow, let us
bring peace and joy to the world.
To do this we must beg God for
His gift of peace and learn to
accept each other as brothers
and sisters, children of God.
We know the best place for
children to learn how to love and
to pray is in the family, by seeing
the love and prayer of their mother
and father. When families are
strongly united, children can see
God's special love in the love of
their father and mother and can
grow to make their country a
loving, prayerful place.

INDEX

INDEX

INDEX

INDEX

INDEX

INDEX

INDEX

INDEX